Co-occurring Substance Abuse and Mental Disorders

D0872911

Co-occurring Substance Abuse and Mental Disorders

A Practitioner's Guide

John Smith

JASON ARONSON
Lanham • Boulder • New York • Toronto • Plymouth, UK

Published in the United States of America
by Jason Aronson
An imprint of Rowman & Littlefield Publishers, Inc.

A wholly owned subsidiary of
The Rowman & Littlefield Publishing Group, Inc.
4501 Forbes Boulevard, Suite 200, Lanham, Maryland 20706
www.rowmanlittlefield.com

Estover Road
Plymouth PL6 7PY
United Kingdom

British Library Cataloguing in Publication Information Available

Library of Congress Cataloging-in-Publication Data

Smith, John, 1956-
    Co-occurring substance abuse and mental disorders: a practitioner's
guide / John Smith.
        p. ; cm.
    Includes bibliographical references and index.
    ISBN-13: 978-0-7657-0452-8 (pbk. : alk. paper)
    ISBN-10: 0-7657-0452-8 (pbk. : alk. paper)
    1. Dual diagnosis.   I. Title.
    [DNLM: 1. Diagnosis, Dual (Psychiatry) 2. Mental Disorders—complications.
    3. Mental Disorders—therapy. 4. Substance-Related Disorders—complications.
    5. Substance-Related Disorders—therapy.
    WM 141 S644c 2007
    RC564.68.S65442 2007
    616.86—dc22   2006026850

Printed in the United States of America

⊗™ The paper used in this publication meets the minimum requirements of American
National Standard for Information Sciences—Permanence of Paper for Printed Library
Materials, ANSI/NISO Z39.48-1992.

Contents

Tables

Introduction

This book is designed for clinicians in either the substance abuse or mental health treatment fields. It is designed as basic training for clinicians who are interested in developing an understanding of co-occurring disorders and their treatment. Readers are cautioned that this is only an overview of the current research and methods on the assessment and treatment of co-occurring disorders. Entire books, courses, and seminars can, and have been, written or conducted in each of the categories presented in this book. Readers are encouraged to read the referenced materials in their entirety and to continue their quest for knowledge in these areas. The literature on co-occurring disorders (aka dual diagnosis) is growing and our knowledge base of the most effective evidence-based treatments is beginning to form; yet the one thing that is constantly recommended in the body of literature currently available is that clinicians become cross-trained in the treatment of these disorders. While there appears to be a growing trend toward integrated treatment of co-occurring disorders, there is still a lack of available training and clinical supervision to assist clinicians in honing and improving their knowledge and skills. Despite overwhelming evidence about the prevalence of co-occurring disorders, the mental health and substance abuse treatment systems have been slow to adapt or respond to the demand for better and more effective treatments for this population. Clinicians have been forced to provide treatment to clients with co-occurring mental illness and substance use disorders without having adequate training or resources to do so. One study by Carey, Purnine, Maisto, Carey, and Simons (2000), showed that clinicians were treating clients with co-occurring disorders, but often felt unprepared and inadequate in their knowledge and skill levels. Surprisingly, these clinicians sought consultation and training whenever available, but cited a lack of training and clinical supervision

1

opportunities as an obstacle to providing quality treatment to these clients. Most clinical training programs and graduate programs in medicine, psychology, social work, addictions, and other related areas offer little, if any, training or course work in the assessment and treatment of co-occurring disorders. Until this occurs, clinicians in all areas will have to get their training and experience on the job and through seminars, books, and other training venues.

This book is designed as both a stand-alone book for the individual clinician or as an adjunct to a group training or seminar. It can be used in conjunction with the clinical vignettes in chapter 7 or in "live" case supervision. Readers are encouraged to share this book and its contents with other clinicians in addition to receiving ongoing clinical supervision.

The following is a sample clinical vignette. The format is such that it allows for a clinical overview followed by a discussion of possible assessment and treatment issues. Readers may find it helpful to develop their own assessments and treatment plans using the evidence-based practices outlined in this book and/or compare their plans to those suggested by the author:

Bill

Bill is a thirty-nine-year-old Caucasian male. Beginning in his late teens, he began to experience social isolation and withdrawal. Originally an average student, his grades declined until he dropped out of high school at seventeen. His circle of friends dwindled as he became more and more isolated. He spent more and more time confined in his room listening to his music and drawing. During this time he also started drinking and smoking pot. He felt that it enhanced his "creativity." His parents both worked long hours and although concerned about Bill, they did nothing to intervene. Whenever they did express concern, Bill would become argumentative and retreat to his room. By his early twenties his alcohol and drug use had increased. In addition to pot he also started using cocaine. He liked how it gave him more energy and "enhanced his creativity." During this time Bill began to require less and less sleep. He would often stay up all night long and then sleep for a few hours during the day. His drawings became more "bizarre." He began to believe that his drawings were "inspired by God." Eventually he began to hear "voices from Heaven" that told him what to draw. His parents became more concerned and attempted on several occasions to get him to go to a psychiatrist. Bill refused and became more hostile and argumentative. His alcohol and drug use continued to increase. His behavior became more and more bizarre until one night Bill was arrested while running nude down the street. He was detained on a seventy-two hour emergency hold and taken to a hospital for psychiatric evaluation. He was diagnosed with schizoaffective disorder. Because his condition was serious enough to warrant an extended hold, he was able to remain hospitalized long enough to begin a medication regimen that helped to stabilize his psychiatric symptoms. His sleeping patterns began to return to normal, and his psychotic symptoms began to diminish. Upon discharge Bill was referred to a local mental health clinic for follow-up treatment. For a while he kept his appointments and took his medications. He was even able to get a job in a warehouse. This allowed him to find a small apartment. He continued to drink alcohol and smoke pot, but his use had lessened. He did not mention that he used alcohol or drugs to his therapist or doctor, and they did not ask him about his substance use. Because he was doing so well, his visits to the clinic were reduced to one time per month. Bill did not like the fact that his medications had caused him to gain a great deal of weight and caused some other unpleasant side effects. He began to think that he was doing so well that he no longer needed the medications. Soon he convinced himself to stop taking the medications. It was not long before his symptoms began to reappear. His sleeping patterns became disrupted. He started to use alcohol and pot heavily to help him sleep. This caused him to miss work. He began to withdraw and again focus on his drawing. His behavior started to become bizarre, and as a result he was fired from his job. Bill did not keep his appointments at the clinic; however, because of his therapist's large caseload there was no attempt to follow up with him. He was subsequently evicted from his apartment and was forced to live on the street in his car. He got a small amount of money from selling pot that he used to buy more pot and alcohol. By now his alcohol use had increased to the point of daily intoxication. It was not long before Bill was arrested for driving under the influence. As part of his sentence Bill was to enter alcohol rehabilitation. Unfortunately his behavior was too bizarre to be admitted to the substance abuse treatment center. They required him to have his psychiatric symptoms stabilized before they could treat his alcohol "problem." They referred back to the mental health clinic, which refused to take him back for treatment until he had been "detoxified." Bill was eventually rehospitalized in the psychiatric unit of a local hospital when they agreed to manage the detoxification. Bill's first few days in the hospital were rough. He became extremely psychotic and agitated, requiring seclusion and restraint. He needed large amounts of medications to manage his withdrawal from alcohol and to stabilize his psychosis. By the time he was released from the hospital, he was still experiencing a significant amount of anxiety, and his sleep patterns were not yet regulated. He continued to experience rapid and pressured speech and rapid thoughts (flight of ideas). While lessened, he still was hearing voices, especially at night. Discharge planning was hampered by his lack of stable housing and income. His parents reluctantly agreed to allow him to return home until he stabilized.

After being discharged Bill returned to the mental health clinic. He began attending therapy groups and had his medications checked regularly. While his substance use was never dealt with directly, his therapist thought it would be a good idea for Bill to attend Alcoholics Anonymous meetings and encouraged him to avoid alcohol as it might interfere with his medications. Bill agreed and he began attending AA at a nearby church. He felt very anxious and uncomfortable at these meetings despite being welcomed by the "old-timers." He rarely shared and never socialized with other members despite being invited to "go for coffee" after meetings. At one point Bill shared his mental illness and the fact that he was on several medications. Unfortunately Bill received a lot of negative feedback about his use of medications from some of the "old-timers" who felt that Bill was not really "clean and sober" if he had to use "all of that medication" to feel better. Bill felt guilty and began to question his use of medication. It was not long until Bill stopped taking his medications. In a predictable pattern Bill relapsed in both his mental illness and his use of alcohol and was soon back on the street and without support.

How does Bill's story end? For Bill the story is not yet over. The end has not been written. The answer depends on whether Bill can find the help that he needs for both his mental illness and his addiction to alcohol. The sad truth for many people like Bill with both a mental illness and a substance use problem is that their stories end tragically in death, incarceration, or homelessness. Bill's story is a true story. It exemplifies the plight that those with co-occurring disorders have in navigating systems of care that are designed to treat "problems" and not people. This book will look at how individuals with both a mental illness and substance use disorder can be helped within an integrated program of care utilizing evidence-based treatments that are proven to enhance positive treatment outcomes. We will follow "Bill" and others through an integrated plan of care and demonstrate how these treatment methodologies are applied to various clinical situations.

Assessment & Treatment Issues

Since Bill has relapsed with both his mental illness and substance use, he will likely need to be rehospitalized in order to stabilize his symptoms and detoxify him from alcohol and drug use. This can be done without hospitalization, but given Bill's history and lack of a structured living environment, it is unlikely that this would be an appropriate approach. Given Bill's history of heavy drug and alcohol use, he may be at risk for serious alcohol withdrawal symptoms and would need medical management and supervision for this. In an integrated program the psychiatric and substance use treatment can begin simultaneously.

The initial goal of treatment will be to stabilize his psychiatric symptoms while simultaneously managing any withdrawal symptoms from substance use. This will primarily involve medical management. Once he is stabilized to the point that he can respond to other interventions, further treatment can begin. The next goal will be to complete a thorough biopsychosocial assessment, which will be a key to a successful outcome for Bill. In Bill's case he has never had an integrated assessment. While his psychiatric and substance abuse problems have been assessed and "treated" in different programs at different times, there has not been a coordinated or integrated approach to his care. In our integrated program we would begin by taking a detailed history. In Bill's case we can see that his psychiatric problems likely began in his early teens when his grades began to decline and he dropped out of high school. His social withdrawal and isolation appear to have preceded his alcohol and drug use. We would want to determine if there were any precipitating factors in the onset of his problems. In Bill's case there did not appear to be any history of problems during his earlier childhood nor were there any specific precursors to his problems such as a significant loss or traumatic event. The progressive onset of his social isolation and withdrawal and his preoccupation with his drawings and music highlight the beginnings of his mental illness. His use of drugs and alcohol both enhanced some of his symptoms while suppressing others. As we take a more detailed history we can begin to see that his previous diagnosis of schizoaffective disorder was probably accurate. A complete psychiatric evaluation will help to further determine the accuracy of this diagnosis. There are other possible diagnoses that might fit the symptom profile and should be ruled out. This is important as it will determine the types of medications that should be used in Bill's treatment. His history of multiple hospitalizations and treatment "failures" along with medication compliance issues need to be further evaluated. Bill's alcohol and drug use seems to be related to his level of psychiatric symptomatology. He has experienced long periods of stable functioning with decreased or no substance use when his symptoms were stabilized.

Even though Bill's psychiatric and substance use problems are well documented, it is still important to get a current evaluation of his mental status, health status, alcohol/drug use, and medication history. Also an assessment of his current "readiness" for change and willingness to engage in the treatment process must be conducted. This is especially important for Bill since he has a history of noncompliance with previous treatment. Another factor important in Bill's assessment is his current living situation and social support system. Clearly for Bill, this is a major problem as he is living on the street and has few if any social supports. If this situation is not addressed during his initial treatment phase, it may preclude a successful transition to further treatment.

If Bill's parents are still willing and able to be of support, they will need education and counseling on how to best support Bill without enabling him. They will need to also understand about his need for medications and about his co-occurring disorders.

Once Bill has stabilized enough from any drug and alcohol withdrawal and/or acute psychiatric symptoms, he can begin attending therapy groups and receiving case management support. Since he was assessed to be highly motivated for treatment, he was assigned to cognitive-behavioral and skills training groups, as he was ready for action phase-oriented treatment interventions. Had he been less motivated for treatment or resistant to any part of his recommended treatment, he would have been assigned for motivational interviewing sessions. These could be conducted in a group setting or an individual setting. In a group setting the emphasis of the group would be on education, and interventions would be constructed for those in the "precontemplation" and "contemplation" stages of change. Individual sessions would focus on identifying resistance to the desired change, possibly via a "cost-benefit" analysis. Bill might benefit from some motivational interviewing around his resistance to medication compliance and his continued substance use.

The cognitive-behavioral focused groups would focus on Bill's self-defeating beliefs and behaviors related to both his mental illness and his substance use. For example, Bill believed that his substance use enhanced his creativity. In the past he also held several bizarre and irrational beliefs about himself and others, which could be explored. Identifying "core" and "addictive" beliefs can help in developing relapse prevention strategies and skills. Disease education and management, including education about medication compliance, potential side effects, and possible interactions with substance use will help Bill to understand how to manage his psychiatric symptoms. He will also learn about the importance of medication compliance and how his substance use might interfere with his medications and exacerbate his problems. Learning symptom management skills can help empower Bill to be more responsible and self-reliant in his own care. In the skills training groups Bill will learn skills that he can apply to both his mental illness and substance use problems. Examples would be developing social and interactional skills to deal with his social isolation and withdrawal; drug and alcohol refusal skills; and assertiveness skills to deal with his interactions with others regarding substance use or other issues.

In addition to his therapy groups, Bill will need case management to assist him with obtaining housing and linking him to community-based support groups. Bill would be an ideal candidate for a structured living environment, such as a Sober Living or halfway house that is designed for clients with co-occurring disorders. This is important because many traditional Sober Living homes do not accept clients who are on medications or who have a mental illness. In a similar vein, Bill will need to be linked up with a 12-step or similar support group that is accepting of and sensitive to the needs of members with co-occurring disorders. Remember that Bill was moderately successful in AA until he was convinced to stop taking his medications, which resulted in devastating consequences.

Keeping Bill engaged in the treatment process and continually assessing both his substance use and mental illness symptomatology, medication compliance, and motivation for treatment are critical to his ongoing success. Bill has a tendency toward relapse, especially when things are going well. Early signs of relapse might include missing appointments; medication noncompliance; return of odd or bizarre behavior; increasing social isolation and withdrawal; and decrease in 12-step meeting attendance. Should these occur, then the treatment team can develop a crisis intervention plan to help stabilize Bill before he relapses or requires more restrictive interventions.

Chapter One

What Are Co-occurring Disorders?

Since the 1980s there has been a growing awareness of the high prevalence of coexisting mental and substance use disorders. The emphasis of the body of research and literature has been on the co-occurrence of substance use disorders with severe mental illness (Mueser, Noordsy, Drake, and Fox, 2003). This book will focus on the screening, assessment, and treatment of persons with co-occurring substance use disorders and severe mental illnesses (dual diagnosis) such as affective disorders (major depression and bipolar disorders); psychotic disorders (schizophrenia and schizoaffective disorder); anxiety disorders (panic disorder, obsessive-compulsive disorder, and posttraumatic stress disorder), and personality disorders (borderline and antisocial). While all mental disorders can co-occur with a substance use disorder, the most prevalent and most severe disorders will be the focus of this book.

Drake and Wallach (2000) point out that:

> the population of persons with co-occurring mental illness and substance use disorders . . . includes individuals with less disabling mental illnesses such as anxiety disorders, those with different severe illnesses such as schizophrenia and bipolar disorder, and those with either substance abuse or substance dependence. (1126–29)

WHAT IS THE PREVALENCE OF CO-OCCURRING DISORDERS?

Several epidemiological studies have been conducted over the last fifteen years or so that have examined the prevalence rates for co-occurring disorders. One of the most extensive studies to date was the Epidemiological Catchment Area (ECA) study (Reiger, Farmer, Rae, Lacke, Keith, Judd, and

Goodwin, 1990). In short, it was estimated that 16.7 percent of the general population suffer from a substance abuse/substance dependence diagnosis in their lifetime. Persons with a DSM-III psychiatric disorder were three to five times as likely to have a substance abuse/dependence disorder. Certain mental disorders had the highest rates of comorbidity. Schizophrenics were estimated to have a 47 percent prevalence rate of substance abuse/dependence. People with affective (mood) disorders had a 32 percent prevalence rate, with the subset of those with bipolar disorder having a 56.1 percent prevalence rate. Individuals diagnosed with anxiety disorders had a 23.7 percent prevalence rate with the panic disorder subset having 35.8 percent comorbidity and those with obsessive-compulsive disorder having a 32.8 percent rate. This study also reported that as many as 80 percent of the patients seeking treatment for an alcohol disorder report distress from psychiatric symptoms, most commonly depressive symptoms. Myrick and his colleagues (2004) report that the ECA study found an estimated 45 percent of individuals with an alcohol use disorder and 72 percent of individuals with a drug use disorder had at least one co-occurring psychiatric disorder.

Another large epidemiological survey (The National Comorbidity Survey) conducted more recently yielded similar results (Kessler, Crum, Warner, Nelson, Schulenberg, and Anthony, 1997). It found that 42.7 percent of individuals with an addictive disorder in a twelve-month period had at least one mental disorder during the same period. Also, 14.7 percent of individuals with a mental disorder had at least one addictive disorder in that same twelve-month period. Individuals with mania were 8.4 times more likely to have lifetime drug dependence than compared to the general population. A more recent article from the same author (Kessler, 2004), suggested that approximately 50 percent of individuals with substance abuse disorders have a comorbid mental illness and that the great majority of those individuals are not receiving any treatment for either disorder. Another study found the prevalence of comorbid affective or anxiety disorders in one hundred men and women seeking substance abuse treatment for cocaine and alcohol abuse to be 48 percent and 70 percent, respectively (Brady, Grice, Dustan, and Randall, 1993). A significant finding in this study was the gender difference in the prevalence of post-traumatic stress disorder (PTSD). Brady and his colleagues found that 46 percent of the women in the study (n=50) suffered from comorbid PTSD compared to 24 percent of the men. A more recent study yielded similar results (Brady, Killeen, Brewerton, and Lucerini, 2000). Finally, a strong relationship exists between antisocial personality disorder and substance abuse (Reiger et al., 1990). There seems to be evidence suggesting that antisocial personality disorder is a common factor accounting for at least some of the high rates of comorbidity of substance abuse in individuals with severe mental illness (Mueser et al., 2003). These researchers also suggest that their findings are consistent with the observation that antisocial personality disorder is more common in persons with dual disorders than in clients with only a mental illness and no substance abuse problems (Mueser, Rosenberg, Drake, Miles, Wolford, Vidaves, et al., 1999).

Clearly, there is a high prevalence of co-occurring substance use disorders in persons with severe mental illness. It is unclear why there is such high co-morbidity, especially with certain disorders (schizophrenia and bipolar disorder). There is no definitive cause-effect relationship, however the existence of antisocial personality disorder as a common factor and the possible biological supersensitivity of persons with severe mental illness to the effects of alcohol and drugs seem to be supported by research (Mueser et al., 2003; Drake and Wallach, 1993). Interestingly, the commonly held belief that persons with co-occurring disorders are self-medicating is not supported by the research, although Mueser and his colleagues point out that some individuals do use alcohol and drugs to deal with dysphoria and other social problems.

TREATMENT MODELS FOR CO-OCCURRING DISORDERS

While the above research shows a high prevalence of co-occurring substance abuse in persons with severe mental illness (approximately 50 percent), many of these individuals do not receive appropriate treatment for either disorder. This is due, in part, to the fragmentation of the treatment delivery systems in the United States. Historically, treatment for mental illness has been provided by the mental health treatment system, and treatment for substance abuse has fallen under the substance abuse treatment system. Coordination and collaboration between these systems has been poor, and individuals with coexisting problems had to receive treatment for each problem via separate and parallel systems (Drake, Essock, Shaner, Carey, Minkoff, and Kola, 2001; Ridgely, Osher, Goldman, and Talbott, 1987). Traditionally, it was thought that these problems should be treated sequentially (e.g., treating the mental illness first, then the substance abuse or vice versa). This philosophy was often the result of administrative or funding issues making persons with either mental illness or substance use disorders ineligible to receive treatment in one system until their symptoms stabilized or were resolved (Mueser et al., 2003; Kavanaugh, Greenway, Jenner, Saunders, White, Sorban, et al., 2000). This approach has been shown to produce poor outcomes for persons with dual disorders (Drake, Mueser, Brunette, and McHugo, 2004; Ziedonis, 2004; Carey et al., 2000). Often, the untreated problems would worsen the treated disorder or make it impossible to treat one disorder without simultaneously treating the other. There was also disagreement about which disorder to treat first (Mueser et al., 2003).

An alternative approach is that of parallel treatment. In this approach, mental illness and substance abuse problems are treated simultaneously but by professionals in different agencies or systems. This approach has also demonstrated poor outcomes because of the problems of communication and collaboration addressed above and because of the different philosophies of treatment in the mental health and substance abuse systems (Ries and Consensus Panel, 1994). For example, the traditional approach to treating substance abuse disorders is to utilize direct confrontation and emotionally charged interventions that may cause persons with certain disorders (e.g., schizophrenia) to experience an exacerbation of their psychiatric symptoms. This type of intervention may also result in the client's withdrawing from treatment or requiring additional psychiatric care (Mueser and McGurk, 2004; Bellack and Gearon, 1998). Also, individuals receiving treatment from a parallel system are often required to navigate the complex systems of care on their own and therefore fail to follow through or become frustrated and unable to establish relationships with treatment providers. This is especially true for individuals who are poorly motivated or who are symptomatically impaired.

The approach that seems to have the best outcomes and is the best suited for those with co-occurring disorders is the integrated treatment approach. There is an increasing body of research supporting the use of this approach for treatment of co-occurring disorders (Ziedonis, 2004; Drake et al., 2004; Goldsmith and Garlapati, 2004; Mueser et al., 2003; Granholm, Anthenelli, Monterio, Sevicile, and Stoler, 2003; Minkoff, 1989, 2000). Integrated treatment consists of combining treatments for substance abuse and mental illness in a coordinated manner within the same treatment relationship or setting. Rather than being program focused, the treatment seeks to be more individualized and tailored to the whole person rather than the type of disorder. This approach has shown favorable outcomes in reducing substance abuse and improving other areas of a person's functioning over nonintegrated approaches to dual disorder treatment (Barrowclough, Haddock, Tarrier, Lewis, Moring, O'Brien, et al., 2001). According to Drake et al. (2001), "integration involves not only combining appropriate treatments for both disorders but also modifying interventions. For example, social skills training emphasize the importance of developing relationships but also the need to avoid social situations that could lead to substance abuse." (470). Changing the pace and philosophical approach of traditional substance abuse treatment to account for the cognitive deficits, vulnerability to confrontation, and negative symptoms of some mental disorders is also recommended (Minkoff, 2000; Bellack and DiClemente, 1999). Other studies have identified several evidence-based practices and program components that must be implemented in order to achieve favorable treatment outcomes (Mueser, Torrey, Lynde, Singer, and Drake, 2003; Drake et al., 2001). To begin, Dr. Kenneth Minkoff (2000) identifies seven "principles of treatment" for people with co-occurring psychiatric and substance abuse disorders.

These are as follows:

I. Comorbidity is an expectation, not an exception.
II. Successful treatment requires most importantly the creation of welcoming, empathic, hopeful, continuous treatment relationships, in which integrated treatment and coordination of care are sustained through multiple treatment episodes.
III. Within the context of the continuous integrated treatment relationship, case management and caretaking must be balanced with empathic detachment and confrontation in accordance with the individual's level of functioning, disability, and capacity for treatment adherence.
IV. When mental illness and substance disorder coexist, both disorders should be considered primary, and integrated dual primary treatment is required.
V. Both psychiatric illnesses and substance dependence are examples of chronic, biological mental illnesses, which can be understood using a disease and recovery model. Each disorder is characterized by parallel phases of recovery: acute stabilization, engagement and motivational enhancement, active treatment and prolonged stabilization, rehabilitation, and recovery.
VI. There is no single correct dual diagnosis intervention. Appropriate practice guidelines require that interventions must be individualized according to the subtype of dual disorder, specific diagnosis of each disorder, phase of recovery/stage of change, and level of functional capacity or disability.
VII. Within a managed-care system, any of the individualized phase-specific interventions can be applied at any level of care. Consequently, a separate multidimensional level of care assessment is required. (252–55)

Clearly, the consensus seems to be that integrated treatment of co-occurring disorders is the best way to achieve positive outcomes and is the recommended form of treatment (CSAT, 2004; Ziedonis, 2004; Drake et al., 2003; Drake and Wallach, 2000; RachBeisel, Scott, and Dixon, 1999). Some authors caution that while the evidence supports integrated treatment, more controlled studies are needed (Drake et al., 2004).

There has been a significant amount of research on the components of effective integrated treatment programs. This research has found that the following components must be present in a program in order to produce the same outcomes:

- Provide stage-wise treatments. Based upon the stages of change developed by Prochaska and DiClemente (1984), programs should tailor interventions to the person's stage of treatment or recovery (Osher and Kofoed, 1989). These stages of treatment include engagement, persuasion/motivation, active treatment, and relapse prevention. The stages of change are precontemplation, contemplation, preparation, action, and maintenance.
- Use motivational interventions to help the client recognize the effects of substance abuse and to develop the desire to change the behaviors supporting this abuse. These interventions are based upon the concepts and practices of motivational interviewing outlined by Miller and Rollnick (2002).
- Establish cognitive-behavioral interventions (Beck, Wright, Newman, and Liese, 1993) including psychoeducation, social skills training (Mueser et al., 2003; Bellack, Mueser, Gingerich, and Agresta, 1997), and relapse prevention.
- Retain clients long term. Clients who remain in treatment for longer intervals achieve better outcomes. Programs must be flexible enough to manage relapses without dismissals in order to prolong retention (Drake et al., 2004).
- Include modified 12-step (Brooks and Penn, 2003; Jerrell and Ridgely, 1999) and community support programs (e.g., Double Trouble) that recognize and accept persons with dual disorders and their special needs (e.g., need to be on psychotropic medications and acceptance of abstinence as a goal vs. an absolute).

Other evidence-based practices (EBPs) for people with severe mental illness (including those with co-occurring substance abuse) identified by Mueser and his colleagues (2003) are collaborative pharmacology, assertive community treatment, family psychoeducation, supported employment, illness management and recovery, and integrated dual disorders treatment. The implementation of these EBPs was also supported by Drake and his colleagues (2001). Many of the above listed practices will be discussed in greater detail later in this book.

BARRIERS TO IMPLEMENTATION OF EVIDENCED-BASED PRACTICES FOR TREATMENT OF CO-OCCURRING DISORDERS

While the literature is supportive of the use of evidence-based practices, there are numerous obstacles to their implementation. In short, these are comprised of policy barriers, program barriers, clinical barriers, consumer barriers, and family barriers. While all of these barriers present formidable obstacles, this book will focus on the clinical barriers that exist. The major clinical obstacles center around two primary areas: philosophical differences and lack of specific training in integrated treatment.

In spite of numerous studies citing the high prevalence of co-occurring substance abuse disorders in persons with severe mental illness and in spite of an equally high number of studies (cited earlier in this book) supporting the implementation of an integrated approach to treating these disorders, surprisingly little has been done to develop and train substance abuse and mental health professionals in these evidenced based practices. For example, Ries and his colleagues (1994) report that different treatment "systems" have different clinical approaches. The mental health system traditionally offers services from professionals from a variety of disciplines, including psychiatrists, psychologists, social workers, registered nurses, and other professional and paraprofessional staff. They offer a wide array of programs and services. Various psychotherapeutic theories and techniques are utilized in a wide range of settings, including the use of psychotropic medications.

A serious limitation for persons with co-occurring disorders is that most clinicians in mental health settings lack skills and knowledge about specific drugs of abuse and the biopsychosocial processes of abuse and addiction: AOD treatment, recovery, and relapse. Similarly, clinicians working in the substance abuse treatment system utilize a wide variety of treatment approaches in a variety of settings.

According to Ries and his colleagues:

> The strengths of addiction treatment services include the multidisciplinary team approach with a biopsychosocial emphasis, and an understanding of the addictive process combined with knowledge of the drugs of abuse and the 12-step programs . . . however few medications that directly treat or interrupt the addictive process have been identified or regularly used. Most addiction treatment professionals attempt to eliminate patients' use of all drugs. (chapter 3, 3)

Clearly, this philosophical difference can be problematic with persons who have a co-occurring severe mental illness requiring certain medications to treat and stabilize their psychiatric symptoms. Ries et al. (1994) highlight this point:

> Many who work in the addiction treatment field have only a limited understanding of medications used for psychiatric disorders. Historically, some people have mistakenly assumed that all or most psychiatric medications are psychoactive or potentially addictive. Many staff have a lack of training and

experience in the use of such medications. In the treatment of dual disorders, a balance must be made between behavioral interventions and the appropriate use of such medications. (chapter 3, 3–4)

The authors also emphasize the need for flexibility toward the goal of abstinence from the use of drugs and alcohol in persons with severe mental illnesses such as schizophrenia. They point out that within parts of the addiction treatment system, abstinence from psychoactive drugs is a precondition to participate in treatment. This precondition could hinder or discourage clients with dual disorders from engaging in the treatment process.

It is this lack of and need for training that is highlighted throughout the research. Mueser et al. (2003) state that:

Dual-diagnosis training must be the centerpiece of a new dual disorder program. All clinicians should be trained in the fundamentals of assessing substance use disorders in clients with severe mental illness, as well as the basic principles of treatment . . . all clinicians need to master certain basic skills, including assessment, motivational-interviewing, and cognitive-behavioral substance abuse counseling. (39)

Other researchers also highlight the need for knowledge and training in treating comorbid cases. Kessler (2004) states that "there is a shortage of adequately trained professionals to deliver these treatments and there is a shortage of treatment settings that provide integrated treatment of dual diagnosis" (733). Drake et al. (2001) state that:

Clinicians trained in substance abuse treatments, as well as recovering dual diagnosis clients could add expertise and training, but they are often excluded from jobs in the mental health system. (473)

Ziedonis (2004) reports that:

Traditional mental health and addiction treatments have not adequately addressed these co-occurring disorders due to clinical interventions, programs, and system flaws that have not addressed the individual's needs. Integrated treatment requires both an understanding of mental illness and addiction and the means to integrate and modify the traditional treatment approaches in both the mental health and addiction treatment fields . . . all mental health clinicians should become experienced and skilled in the core psychotherapy approaches to treating substance use disorders, including motivational enhancement therapy, relapse prevention (cognitive-behavioral therapy), and 12-step facilitation. In addition, integrated treatment includes integrating medications for both addiction and mental illness with the behavioral therapies and other psychosocial interventions. (892–904)

In their review of systems problems in contemporary addiction treatment, McLellan and Meyers (2004) report that "there has been little effort to train key personnel from these systems (e.g., mental health case workers, probation officers) in the use of some of the proven substance abuse screening instruments" (766). They also report that in a study by the National Association of State Alcohol and Drug Abuse Directors (2002), the mental health system was not even recorded as a major purchaser of substance abuse treatment. McLellan and Meyers (2004) also state that:

> There is a need for training to recognize the signs of alcohol/drug abuse or dependence. Professional courses in undergraduate and graduate education, state qualification examinations that include a set of identification-related questions, in-service programs, and orientation of new staff members would help in this effort. (766)

Lastly, Gassman, Demone, and Albilal (2001) report on attempts to incorporate training on substance abuse assessment and other alcohol and drug content in courses offered to graduate social work students. Currently, most training programs for mental health, substance abuse, and medical professional offer little or no cross-training in the identification, assessment, and treatment of co-occurring disorders (Marshall, 2004; Maslin, 2001; Carey et al., 2000).

This book is designed to provide basic training to both mental health and substance abuse professionals in the identification, assessment, and treatment of co-occurring substance use disorders and severe mental illness. An emphasis will be made on the use of evidence-based practices and techniques.

Chapter Two

Assessment of Co-occurring Disorders

Both the substance abuse and mental health treatment systems emphasize the importance of completing a comprehensive assessment of clients entering treatment. This assessment should focus on all aspects of an individual's functioning. An assessment that looks at a person's biological or health history and status; psychological or mental health history and status; and their social history and status, a biopsychosocial assessment, is recommended. When working with co-occurring disorders, we are looking for data that will help the clinician make an accurate assessment and diagnosis of both types of disorders. Since symptoms of substance abuse and mental illness can mimic one another, it is critically important to get historical information on a person's psychological functioning and on their substance use history. Initially, it may be difficult to determine if a client's symptoms are the result of a mental illness or of a substance use disorder or both. Albanese and Pies (2004) provide clinicians with a basic list of circumstances in which the clinician should be suspicious of a substance-induced psychiatric presentation. These include the following:

- first occurrence of psychiatric symptoms happens at an older age (since primary psychiatric disorders typically have an age of onset within the first few decades of life);
- abrupt onset of psychiatric symptoms;
- no family history of psychiatric illness (a family history of psychiatric disorder is suggestive of the presence of a primary psychiatric diagnosis);
- unusual presentation in a known psychiatric patient;
- resolution of psychiatric symptoms over a period of one to three weeks;
- the presence of physiological signs such as autonomic instability and pupillary constriction or dilation (a positive urine or drug screen indicating the presence of substances in the individual is also an indicator).

We will examine some of the basic components that should be included in this type of assessment:

MEDICAL/HEALTH SCREENING

There are several reasons why a basic medical and health screening is necessary. First, all mental health disorders can be caused by problems related to a medical condition. The American Psychiatric Association's *Diagnostic and Statistical Manual of Mental Disorders,* fourth edition, text revision (DSM-IV-TR) (2000), requires clinicians to screen for disorders that are due to a general medical condition. While the determination of a person's general medical condition may require an examination by a physician, it is always appropriate for the clinician to determine if a person has any current or historical medical conditions. Often this is accomplished by having the client complete a brief health-screening questionnaire describing any current or past medical problems. Sudden changes in a person's mental status could be indicative of an undiagnosed or untreated medical condition. This is especially true in middle-aged and older adults. Second, all symptoms of mental disorders can be caused by alcohol or drug use, intoxication, or withdrawal. For example, is a client who is delusional and hallucinating suffering from schizophrenia or from delirium tremens (DTs), a serious and potentially life threatening medical condition brought on by alcohol withdrawal? Failure to identify and treat the alcohol withdrawal could put this client at risk. Third, people with serious mental illness and people with serious substance use disorders do not take adequate care of themselves and their health. They are at risk for a host of diseases and problems related to their lifestyle and to their specific disorder(s). For example, long-term alcohol abuse is associated with a host of serious medical conditions including heart disease, high blood pressure, diabetes, and more. People with serious mental illness and co-occurring substance abuse are at higher risk for serious infections such as HIV or hepatitis A-C (Drake et al., 2004). There should always be a basic screening for all communicable diseases, such as HIV; hepatitis A, B, and C; and tuberculosis (TB). Given the high risk behaviors (needle sharing, unprotected sex, unsanitary conditions, lack of health care) engaged in by clients with these conditions, a general screening should always be conducted. As an aside, all clinicians should be trained in the use of universal precautions and assume that every client is potentially infected with one of these infectious disorders, especially if they come into contact with body fluids or secretions.

Because of the poor health status of many clients with co-occurring disorders, it is important to ascertain when they received their most recent medical examination. If it has been a long time (e.g., greater than two years) or if there is any indication that the client has any current medical condition or may be at risk (e.g., has previously experienced severe withdrawal symptoms including seizures when withdrawing from alcohol), then the client should be examined by a physician as soon as possible. Depending on the treatment setting and/or level of care, many programs require clients to receive a physical examination upon admission. This may not be the case with most outpatient mental health or substance abuse treatment programs. It is, therefore, up to the clinician assessing the client to make the decision to have a medical exam performed. One reason why it is recommended that integrated treatment programs utilize a multidisciplinary team approach to treat co-occurring disorders is that staff trained in medical/health assessment are available (Goldsmith and Garlapati, 2004; Granholm et al., 2003).

For obvious reasons, it is necessary to obtain an accurate list of any current and recent medications, including psychotropics. This will alert the clinician to any current or recent health and/or psychiatric problems the client may have experienced. This is a good opportunity for the clinician to ask about medication compliance, the client's response to medications, adverse side effects, and medication history (e.g., how long has the client been on this medication and has he ever been treated for this same condition with any other medication). Unfortunately, many clients with co-occurring disorders are poor historians due to their psychiatric symptomatology and/or their substance use impairments. Information from collateral sources, such as family members or other treatment providers, can be beneficial in these cases. Without this information, treatment could be delayed and problems could be exacerbated. This should be done in accordance with all applicable confidentiality laws (Center for Substance Abuse Treatment, 2004). A more detailed overview of commonly prescribed psychiatric medications will be presented later in this book.

DETAILED ALCOHOL/DRUG USE HISTORY

This is the part that is often overlooked or inadequately assessed. Mueser et al. (2003) state that "the most significant obstacle to assessing substance abuse in clients with psychiatric disorders is the failure to take a proper history of the client's use of alcohol and drugs" (52). This is often because the clinician fails to ask clients about their use of substances. Mueser and his colleagues suggest that it is helpful to begin talking about the client's past substance use first and then move gradually toward more recent use. This is felt to reduce client defensiveness. The authors also point out that it is common for individuals with substance abuse problems to deny or minimize their use and the negative effects of this use, as well as the extent of their mental illness and the subsequent impairments from both disorders. There are numerous examples of forms that can be used for obtaining a detailed substance use history. There are also numerous assessment tools/instruments. Some of these will be reviewed and discussed later in this book. Generally, the following information is included:

- Specific substances used. Clinician should ask specific questions about each substance. For example, ask about alcohol, marijuana, cocaine, LSD, and others.
- Age of first use of each substance.
- Frequency and amount of each substance used. Also track the progression of use from past to present. (e.g., "So your marijuana use went from once or twice a week on weekends beginning at fifteen to daily use from age twenty to present.")
- Route of administration (typically drink, smoke, snort, or intravenous).
- Longest period of abstinence or sobriety (past and most recent).
- Consequences of use. Physical signs of abuse/dependence such as blackouts, loss of control, increased tolerance, history of withdrawal symptoms, and compulsive use. Legal, social, and medical consequences are also important. (It is common for clients with substance use disorders to not always be aware of or acknowledge that there have been any negative consequences from their use of substances.)

PSYCHOLOGICAL HISTORY AND FUNCTIONING

Substance abuse counselors do not assess clients for mental illnesses almost as often as mental health counselors fail to assess for substance use problems. As previously discussed, this is due to a lack of education and training. Screening for the presence of psychological problems is made even more difficult by the fact that almost every psychological symptom can be mimicked by the use of alcohol or drugs. It makes the job of assessment more difficult for the clinician. This is one reason to get an accurate account of the client's history of psychological functioning.

The clinician should begin with questions about any prior treatment for a psychiatric or an emotional problem. This phrase is used specifically because most clients will understand what this means. A more clinical term like "mental disorder" might be misunderstood by the client. The clinician should also keep in mind that having prior treatment or having a previous psychiatric diagnosis does not automatically mean that the client has a mental illness. Many an untrained clinician has misdiagnosed a substance use disorder as depression or has failed to identify the co-occurrence of both disorders leading to treatment for one disorder but not for the other. Nonetheless, the default position for the clinician should be that a previous history or diagnosis of a psychiatric or emotional disorder is a strong indicator for the existence of a co-occurring disorder. Further questioning as to when the treatment was received, previous hospitalizations, medications, and the client's response to medications should follow. Even if the client denies any prior history of mental health treatment, it is still important for the clinician to assess the client's current psychological functioning. This is best done through a clinical interview called a Mental Status Examination or MSE (Donnelly, Rosenbert, Fleeson, 1970). While there are several versions of this examination, every clinician can use some common elements when interviewing and assessing a client's current psychological functioning. These are:

- Appearance: General appearance (mode of dress appropriate/inappropriate to situation, weather, etc.); unkempt vs. well groomed; hygiene, posture, and motor activity; and eye contact; anything unusual about the way the client looks.
- Affect: General mood or tone (elated, depressed, flat, or expressive); speech (rapid, pressured, slow, deliberate, or slurred); hostile or withdrawn; nervous or anxious; labile or appropriate to situation.
- Thought Process: This is the flow of thoughts vs. the content that will also be important. Generally we will look at how the thoughts string together in a logical and sequential manner vs. an illogical or incoherent manner. Does the client make sense and/or respond appropriately? Do the thoughts relate to one another, or are they loosely associated (e.g., two thoughts do not directly relate to one another)? Are the thoughts coming too rapidly for the client to keep up with (racing), or does the client change topics often (flight of ideas)? Are the thoughts filled with unnecessary detail or vagueness (circumstantiality)? Does the client branch off of the main topic never getting to the point (tangentiality)?
- Thought Content: What is the main focus of the client's thoughts? Are there preoccupations with any particular subject? Are there any delusions (paranoid, persecutory, grandiose) or ideas of reference (belief that everything refers to them)? Are there any intrusive or compulsive (repetitive) thoughts? Are there any hallucinations (auditory, visual, olfactory, tactile) or unexplained sensations? Are there any obsessions or compulsions? Any unreasonable fears (phobias)?

- Risk Assessment: Does the client have any suicidal thoughts or plans? Is the client having any thoughts of hurting himself or herself? Does the client have a plan for or thinking about committing suicide? If the client has a plan, does he or she have access to the method? Has the client ever attempted suicide before? A similar line of questioning should be done to assess for violence potential. (Does the client have any homicidal or violent thoughts or plans?) Clients with co-occurring disorders are at a greater risk for suicide and violence than others, and the potential for self-harm and harm to others should continuously be assessed. Every clinician should be aware of demographic and other risk factors associated with suicide and homicide/violence potential. Some basic assessment questions for suicide risk are:

—Is the client having any thoughts of suicide or self-harm?
—Has the client thought or planned how to kill himself or herself?
—Does the client have a method or a means and access to it?
—Has the client ever attempted suicide before?
—Has the client engaged in any recent behavior that would indicate that he or she was planning suicide?

The answers to these questions will help the clinician determine the risk potential for suicide or self-harm. For example, asking the client directly about suicidal thoughts is the best way to ascertain if the client is having any ideation. Many clinicians are mistakenly uncomfortable asking a client this question directly because they fear that they will cause the client to start thinking about suicide. Most experts on suicidality agree that allowing a client to ventilate feelings about suicide is often helpful in alleviating the client's suicidal feelings and impulses. Not all clients are truthful or able to identify suicidal thoughts or feelings, so the clinician should always rely on his or her instincts to assess risk. Clients may have suicidal thoughts and feelings but do not intend to act on them. If the client is able to articulate a specific plan or method and he or she has access to that method, the clinician should consider the client to be at high risk for suicide. Also, if a client has a history of previous suicide attempts (treated or untreated), they should also be considered at high risk. Most people who complete suicide have attempted suicide at least once before they are successful. Homicidal or violent feelings/thoughts can be assessed by asking similar questions. Ultimately, the clinician must make a clinical judgment about the level of suicide/homicide/violence risk that the client presents. Clinicians should be aware of the laws pertaining to their duty to warn and protect, involuntary commitment, and of policies and procedures to manage clients who are a danger to themselves and/or others.

- Memory, Cognition, and Orientation: Probably one of the best ways to assess these areas is to perform the Mini-Mental Status Examination or MMSE (Folstein, Folstein, and McHugh, 1973). In general, the clinician is attempting to determine how well the client can process and recall information. Cognitive impairments are common among individuals with co-occurring disorders. This is due to the nature of certain mental disorders, such as schizophrenia, and to impairments secondary to substance use and intoxication. These impairments can also be present in individuals with organic brain disorders, such as Alzheimer's and other dementias. In short, the clinician should determine the client's level of consciousness. Are they confused, alert, and oriented to person, place, time, and situation? The client's memory should be tested by asking the client to remember three common words made up by the clinician (e.g., tree, dog, and automobile) and asking him or her to repeat them a few minutes later. Ask the client to spell the word "world" forwards and backwards. Ask the client the name of a first grade teacher. Ask the client what he or she watched on television yesterday. The answers to these questions should give the clinician a good idea of the client's basic cognitive functioning and memory.
- Insight: Do the clients have an awareness of or acknowledge having a mental illness and/or a substance abuse problem? Do they acknowledge or recognize any negative consequences or impairments in functioning? Do they deny, rationalize, or blame others for their problems?
- Judgment: Assess the clients' current and past histories of using appropriate judgment in various situations. Do they have a logical plan for approaching their situation? Do they have a history of making appropriate decisions in similar situations? Is their judgment or thinking impaired due to the use of substances or their psychiatric symptoms?
- Impulse Control: Do the clients have the ability to control their behavior, or are they reacting to impulses? Are they likely to be able to react and respond appropriately to a given situation?

The significance of the MSE is that it will give the clinician a fairly good idea of the client's current and recent level of psychological functioning. From this, the clinician can determine if the client has any symptoms that might indicate a mental illness or psychiatric condition that could be secondary to substance use. For example, if the client is experiencing a high degree of suspicion and paranoia, he or she may be experiencing psychosis related to schizophrenia, bipolar disorder, a substance use disorder (e.g., methamphetamine psychosis), or some other condition. The specific diagnosis is of less immediate concern to the clinician than the need to have this client evaluated further and/or treated for his or her symptoms.

• History of Trauma and Abuse: Many clients with co-occurring disorders have been the victims of trauma and/or abuse during their lives, either as children, adults, or both. As previously stated, there is a high prevalence of post-traumatic stress disorder (PTSD) among individuals with co-occurring disorders. According to CSAT (2004) the rate of PTSD among people with substance abuse disorders is between 12 and 34 percent. It may be as high as 60 to 75 percent for women with substance abuse disorders (Brady, 2000). CSAT reports that people with PTSD and substance abuse are more likely to experience further trauma than people with substance abuse alone. They also report that people with PTSD tend to abuse the most serious substances (cocaine and opioids); however abuse of prescription medications, marijuana, and alcohol are common. In addition, because of the possibility of repeated trauma in domestic violence, child abuse, rape, and other situations related to substance-using lifestyles, the clinician should assess for safety issues and assist the client in developing a safety plan to avoid further trauma/abuse. It is not uncommon for clients to be reluctant or unwilling to reveal current or past trauma/abuse. This may be due to fear of further violence by the abuser, fear that revealing the abuse could cause additional problems for the client or the abuser (e.g., jail, having children taken away due to child abuse or domestic violence, or loss of living and economic situation), or the inability to recall past abuse and trauma due to repression of memories related to the traumatic event(s). Clinicians should be sensitive when asking clients about trauma/abuse and realize that there might be a previous history that they are unable to reveal or feel uncomfortable discussing. Appropriate questions might include:

—Have you ever been the victim of domestic violence or abuse?
—Do you recall any time when you were hurt or abused by someone?
—Have you ever been concerned for your safety in your marriage/relationship?
—In your family when you were growing up, do you recall any time when anyone hurt or abused you physically or sexually?

If the client denies any history of previous trauma/abuse, the clinician should continue to assess throughout the treatment process. Many times clients will reveal previous incidents of trauma/abuse as they feel more comfortable in the relationship with the clinician. As other clients reveal and discuss their histories of abuse/trauma, the client may recall his or her own history or feel more at ease discussing it with others.

- Social History: This will include a history of social functioning both current and past. "Social" refers to the client's functioning with others and in the community. It usually will encompass the following areas:

  —Family of Origin: This is the family in which the client grew up. Have the client describe his family makeup (father, mother, siblings, stepparent, adopted, etc.). What was it like growing up in that family? Were there any significant issues or problems that the client remembers? Are they all still alive? If not, when and how did they die? Is there a family history of mental illness (treated or untreated) and/or substance abuse? If so, what type of problems (or symptoms) did he/she have? What kind of relationship does the client currently have with his parents and siblings? Are they supportive? Are they estranged and if so, why? Answers to these questions may help give the clinician clues to the existence of co-occurring disorders. Mental illness and substance abuse tend to run in families. If the family history is positive for certain mental illnesses (bipolar disorder, major depression, schizophrenia) or for substance abuse, there is a high probability that the client may have similar problems or be at risk for developing these problems. Also, family of origin issues, especially abuse, is often at the root of many substance use and emotional problems.

  —Marital/Relationship History: Are the clients currently married or in a serious relationship? Have they ever been married before? If so, how long? (When did they divorce? Why did they divorce)? What are their spouses' or partners' reactions to their current problems? Has their spouse/partner ever expressed concern about their substance use? Concern about their behavior? If possible, and within the limits of client confidentiality, it is helpful to interview the spouse/partner or other collateral individuals to get history and pertinent information. This can be compared to the client's self-reported information. Clients may minimize or deny problems, frequency or amount of substance use, and impact on others. This information is vital to the clinician as he/she makes their assessment.

- Legal History: Has the client ever been arrested for any crime, especially crimes related to the possession and use of substances such as driving under the influence (DUI) or public intoxication (PI)? If so, does the client remember his/her BAC (blood alcohol level)? This information can be useful later to help the client see the possible negative consequences resulting from using substances. It may also give the clinician an idea as to the client's tolerance level for certain substances and/or the progression of their addiction. For example, a client with two DUIs and BACs of .120 and .231 respectively, would clearly have an increasingly high tolerance for alcohol. This would show that the client is drinking a large amount of alcohol and experiencing serious consequences legally, financially, and physically from its use.

- Social/Recreational History: Does the client have any close friends? What are his or her social relationships like? What does the client do for fun? Does he or she have any hobbies or engage in any recreational activities? Has the client changed or lost interest in previously enjoyable activities? Has the client changed the types of friends and acquaintances he or she associates with? Do most of the client's activities revolve around substance use? Are the client's acquaintances mostly involved in drug or alcohol use?
- Work/Educational History: Does the client have a history of steady employment or has he or she had unstable employment or frequent job changes? Has the client ever lost a job due to substance use or inappropriate behavior? Is the client currently employed at a level commensurate with their education and ability? What is the highest level of education completed by the client? Were there any problems in school (academically or behaviorally)? Were there any learning disabilities?

Other areas can be assessed as well, such as military history and financial history. Each of the areas listed above help to provide the clinician with a picture of a person's overall functioning in all primary life areas. Impairments in social, occupational, psychological, and physical functioning are considered as diagnostic criteria for most mental and substance use disorders. As the severity and amount of impairments increase, the clinician can determine the existence of co-occurring disorders and the types of interventions that will be necessary to treat the individual client. Typically, the information obtained in these assessments is used to formulate a list of problems to be addressed and to develop a comprehensive treatment plan. This is best done utilizing a multidisciplinary team approach (Granholm et al., 2003). When done in an integrated way, each discipline can insure that it has evaluated the client for the possibility of a co-occurring disorder.

The clinician can also use one of several assessment tools. One of the most commonly used tools is the Addictions Severity Index, or ASI (McLellan, Kushner, Metzger, Peters, Smith, Grissom, et al., 1992). It can be used as an assessment tool for both addictions and mental illness and as a measurement of a client's need for treatment over time. The Beck Depression Inventory-II (BDI-2) is also useful in identifying depressive symptoms (Beck, Steer, and

Brown, 1996). A simple test for alcoholism screening that can be used by all clinicians is the CAGE Questionnaire (Ewing, 1984). Other popular screening tests are the Michigan Alcoholism Screening Test (MAST) developed by Selzer (1971) and the Drug Abuse Screening Test (DAST) developed by Gavin, Ross, and Skinner (1989).

The clinician should become familiar with these and other useful and valid screening tools and measures.

Chapter Three

Major Mental Disorders

SCHIZOPHRENIA AND OTHER PSYCHOTIC DISORDERS

This category of mental disorders is characterized by the prevalence of psychotic features, such as delusions and hallucinations, along with some disturbance in thinking and sometimes mood. It should be noted that psychotic symptoms can also be present in clients with bipolar disorder/mania and/or with major depression. As previously stated, the clinician should always remember that psychotic symptoms could always be induced by drugs and alcohol or be present due to a general medical condition. This is why an accurate history may help the clinician to determine if a mental disorder is present and causing the symptoms and behavior, or if a substance may be the catalyst.

Probably the most prevalent of the psychotic disorders is schizophrenia. The DSM-IV-TR (2000) lists the following diagnostic criteria for schizophrenia:

I. The presence of two or more of the following characteristic symptoms for at least a one month period (although continuous signs of the disturbance must have persisted for at least six months):
   A. delusions
   B. hallucinations
   C. disorganized speech
   D. grossly disorganized or catatonic behavior
   E. negative symptoms
II. One or more major area of functioning (work, interpersonal relations, or self-care) is markedly below levels achieved prior to onset of the disturbance.

III. No evidence of Schizoaffective or Mood Disorders with psychotic fea-
tures. For this to occur there can be no evidence of Major Depressive,
Manic, or Mixed episodes occurring concurrently with active phase
Schizophrenic symptoms (listed under section #1 above). (298–317)

Mueser and McGurk (2004) describe schizophrenia as:

> . . . a major mental illness characterized by psychosis, apathy, and social with-
> drawal, and cognitive impairment, which results in impaired functioning in
> work, school, parenting, self-care, independent living, interpersonal relation-
> ships, and leisure time. Among psychiatric disorders, schizophrenia is the most
> disabling and requires a disproportionate share of mental health services. (2063)

Schizophrenia tends to develop most often between the ages of sixteen and
thirty. Onset after age forty-five is infrequent. This disorder usually has a
gradual onset that takes place over an average of five years, beginning with
the emergence of negative and depressive symptoms. This is followed by
cognitive and social impairment and several years later by the emergence of
psychotic symptoms and, as a result, the first psychiatric contact. Substance
use and/or abuse often begins in the earlier phases and may progress as the
course of the schizophrenia progresses. Mueser and McGurk (2004) describe
the cognitive impairment in schizophrenia as including "problems in attention
and concentration, psychomotor speed, learning and memory, and executive
functions (e.g., abstract thinking, problem solving)" (2064).

There are several subtypes of schizophrenia that are characterized by their
primary symptoms. They are:

• Paranoid type: This type is characterized by the presence of delusions
and/or hallucinations that contain persecutory or suspicious themes (e.g.,
"everyone is out to get me"; "I am being followed"). According to the
American Psychiatric Association's *Diagnostic and Statistical Manual of
Mental Disorders* (DSM-IV-TR 2000), the delusions may also contain
themes of grandiosity, jealousy, religiosity, or somatization. Hallucinations
may contain content related to the above themes (e.g., "I hear voices coming from the ceiling, and they are saying bad things about me."; "I see men
from the FBI in the hallway, and they are after me.") Command type hallucinations (voices that tell the person to do or not do something), especially
those that involve harming themselves or others, should be of special concern to the clinician and should be continuously assessed and monitored.
These kinds of hallucinations, combined with persecutory and grandiose
delusions and anger, may predispose the client to violence and/or suicide

(DSM-IV-TR, 2000). Mueser and McGurk (2004) report that while all forms of hallucinations can occur with schizophrenia, the most common type are auditory hallucinations. Common types of delusions in schizophrenia are the persecutory type, delusions of control (e.g., the belief that others can interfere with one's thoughts), grandiose delusions (e.g., the belief that one is Jesus Christ), and somatic delusions (e.g., the belief that one's brain is rotting away).

- Disorganized type: This type is characterized by disorganized speech, disorganized or bizarre behavior, and flat or inappropriate affect. These are commonly referred to as negative symptoms as compared to hallucinations, delusions, and disorganized thinking that are considered positive symptoms of the disorder. The DSM-IV-TR states that "the behavioral disorganization (i.e., lack of goal orientation) may lead to severe disruption in the ability to perform activities of daily living (e.g., showering, dressing, or preparing meals)" (314).

Mueser and McGurk (2004) report that negative symptoms are:

> Deficit states in which basic emotional and behavioral processes are diminished or absent. Common negative symptoms include blunted affect (e.g., monotonous voice tone), anhedonia (lack of pleasure), avolition or apathy (diminished ability to initiate and follow through on plans), and alogia (reduced quantity or content of speech) . . . and are strongly associated with poor psychosocial functioning. (2064)

- Catatonic type: This type is characterized by motoric immobility (catalepsy or stupor), excessive motor activity, extreme negativism (rigid and bizarre posturing resisting any attempt to be moved or resistance to all instructions), mutism, echolalia (senseless repetition of a word or phrase), or echopraxia (the repetitive imitations of the movements of others). According to the DSM-IV-TR:

> During severe catatonic stupor or excitement, the person may need careful supervision to avoid self harm or harming others. There are potential risks from malnutrition, exhaustion, hyperpyrexia, or self inflicted injury. (315)

- Undifferentiated Type: When the person has some or all of the symptoms (delusions, hallucinations, disorganized speech, disorganized behavior, negative symptoms) but does not fit the criteria for any of the other subtypes, they are classified here.
- Residual Type: If the client has had at least one prior episode of schizophrenia but is not currently experiencing any prominent positive psychotic symptoms, they should be classified within this subtype.

Schizophrenic clients who have a co-occurring substance use disorder and who are in an active phase of their disorder (i.e., experiencing psychotic symptoms) may need to have their symptoms stabilized before their substance abuse can be addressed. It is important, however, to begin addressing the client's substance use as soon as possible because continued substance use will exacerbate the client's mental illness and/or disrupt medication compliance and efficacy. Because of the negative symptoms associated with schizophrenia (e.g., lack of goal orientation and avolition), it may be difficult to engage the client in treatment for either disorder. What may appear as resistance or denial may actually be a manifestation of schizophrenic symptoms.

Both psychotic and substance use disorders are chronic disorders with multiple relapses and remissions requiring long-term treatment (Mueser et al., 2003) and a treatment program philosophy that is based on a multidisciplinary team approach (CSAT, 2004). Mueser and McGurk (2004) delineate that treatment of schizophrenia involves both psychopharmacological and psychosocial treatment. Specific evidence-based psychosocial interventions for treating schizophrenia include:

- assertive community treatment that focuses on engaging patients who do not regularly attend other treatment. Evidence shows that this approach results in reduced symptoms and readmissions, improved housing stability and quality of life, and less cost.
- family psychoeducation that reduces the burden of care on families and increases family support for the patient.
- supported employment that helps patients to obtain and keep competitive work in integrated community settings.
- social skills training with a goal of increasing social skills such as having conversations, making friends, resolving conflict, expressing feelings, assertiveness, and developing leisure and recreational activities. This has been shown to improve social and leisure functioning.
- training in illness management skills that improves the patient's understanding and knowledge of schizophrenia, increases medication compliance, prevents relapses, and reduces distress due to symptoms.
- cognitive-behavior therapy for psychosis aimed at reducing the severity of psychotic symptoms and negative symptoms.
- integrated treatment for comorbid substance abuse that focuses on reduction of harmful consequences of substance abuse. Using motivation based interventions and psychoeducation has been shown to decrease substance abuse.

An earlier study by Barrowclough et al. (2001) examined the outcomes of an integrated treatment program utilizing many of these same components.

They conducted a controlled randomized trial of patients with comorbid psychotic disorders (schizophrenia and schizoaffective disorder) and substance use disorder. The control group received standard treatment, and the experimental group received integrated treatment, including a combination of motivational interviewing, cognitive-behavioral interventions, and family intervention. Routine or standard care, provided to both groups, was defined as psychiatric management/medication management, case management, and access to community-based rehabilitative services. The experimental group showed significant improvement in general functioning, reduction in positive symptoms, and an increase in the percent of number of days abstinent from drugs and alcohol. In a review of research, RachBeisel, Scott, and Dixon (1999) found that integrated treatment of co-occurring severe mental illness and substance use disorders that included harm reduction, treatment in stages, motivational interviewing, cognitive-behavioral interventions, and modified 12-step self-help groups showed the most promise in treating this population.

Bellack and Gearon (1998) described an experimental program for substance-abusing patients with schizophrenia that included several of these components. Their program consisted of the following four treatment modules:

I. Social skills and problem solving training to enable patients to develop nonsubstance using social contacts and be able to refuse social pressure to use substances, as well as increasing self-efficacy for change.
II. Education about the reasons for substance abuse (e.g., habits, triggers, and craving) and the particular dangers of substance use for people with schizophrenia to help switch the decisional balance toward decreased use.
III. Motivational interviewing and goal setting to identify realistic, short-term goals for decreased substance use.
IV. Training in behavioral skills to cope with urges and high-risk situations, and relapse prevention skills.

Additionally, participants were asked to submit to regular urinalysis to help enhance motivation to change and increase goal orientation. It was noted that the sessions were highly structured and repetitive with an emphasis on behavioral rehearsal in order to compensate for cognitive deficits. Sessions were broken down into small units and behavioral skills were practiced in small increments. While abstinence was an ultimate goal, participants were instructed in harm avoidance techniques and were not required to maintain abstinence as a condition of participation. In a follow-up study, the authors showed promising early results using this model and suggested further controlled studies to support this conclusion (Bellack and DiClemente, 1999).

A recent study by Xie, McHugo, Helmstetter, and Drake (in press), three-year recovery outcomes for long-term patients with co-occurring schizophrenic and substance use disorders, showed that patients with either schizophrenia or schizoaffective disorders and a substance use disorder who received integrated dual disorders treatment exhibited mostly favorable outcomes. Significant reductions in the rates of hospitalizations, homelessness, competitive employment, and association with nonsubstance-abusing friends were recorded. They also noted a reduction in substance abuse, with 40 percent of the participants reporting full remission at three years, although most participants experienced relapses of substance abuse during the course of these three years. These results are consistent with a study done by Ho, Tsuang, Liberman, Wang, Wilkins, Eckman, et al. (1999) that looked at the treatment outcomes of 179 patients with chronic psychotic illness (primarily schizophrenia) and a comorbid substance use disorder. These patients were treated in a special day program for dual diagnosis. The authors found that the patients treated in this specialized program were able to show increased treatment engagement in the early phases of the treatment process. This led to decreased hospitalizations in the six months after entering the day treatment program. Also shown was decreased substance abuse and increased abstinence in those patients who completed the program, suggesting that keeping these patients engaged in treatment for a longer period of time produces better substance use outcomes. They attributed the increase in positive outcomes to assertive case management and the increased competency and experience of the staff in treating this special population as the most important contributory factors.

Osher and Kofoed (1989) found that treatment of substance abuse with schizophrenics must be conceptualized as an ongoing process in which the motivation to reduce substance use waxes and wanes over time. These clients need ongoing support provided by programs that are tolerant of patients dropping in and out, abstaining a while only to relapse. Bellack and Gearon (1998) suggest that schizophrenic patients with substance abuse problems are generally unable to make and stand by definitive commitments to become abstinent. They suggest that programs treating this population be flexible in their requirements for abstinence as a condition for entering into or staying in treatment. They recommend motivating clients toward abstinence as the goal as opposed to requiring total abstinence as a condition of participation in treatment. Certain factors related to symptoms of schizophrenia may make motivation to stop using substances an ongoing issue. For example, the negative symptoms of avolition and anenergia may decrease motivation in schizophrenic patients (Ziedonis and Trudeau, 1997). The negative symptom of anhedonia may limit the patient's ability to experience pleasure or positive reinforcement in the abstinence of substance use thereby restricting the patient's ability to identify the advantages of reduced substance use (Bellack and Gearon, 1998). The cognitive deficits previously outlined (Mueser and McGurk, 2004) may interfere with the patient's ability to comprehend complex or abstract concepts, process psychoeducational materials, and cope with heightened emotional content.

While the importance and effectiveness of the 12-step model of substance abuse recovery has been shown to be effective in treating substance use disorders and in treating those with a co-occurring mental illness, several authors caution that the heightened emotionality, confrontational approach, and abstinence requirements may cause persons with severe mental illness (schizophrenia) to be unable to tolerate these groups (Carey et al., 2000; Bellack and Gearon, 1998). In fact, the confrontational, highly affective style of many traditional substance abuse treatments is contraindicated for people with schizophrenia (Bellack and DiClemente, 1999).

More will be discussed on specific treatment techniques in a later chapter. The above information is an abbreviated version of the detailed descriptions included in the DSM-IV-TR (2000). The clinician should become familiar with this reference book as part of their ongoing training and development.

AFFECTIVE DISORDERS

The affective or "mood" disorders are the most prevalent co-occurring disorders. People with bipolar disorder or major depression frequently have a co-occurring substance use disorder (Myrick, Cluver, Swavely, and Peters, 2004). Many people receiving treatment for addiction appear depressed, and during the first months of sobriety, many substance abusers exhibit symptoms of depression (or bipolar) that are related to acute withdrawal or intoxication. Usually, these symptoms will fade over time. Unless the patient has a previous history/treatment of an affective disorder, a period of time should elapse before an affective disorder is diagnosed (Ries and Consensus Panel, 1994). They also suggest that acute manic symptoms can be mimicked or induced by intoxication with stimulants, hallucinogens, or other polysubstance combinations. The treatment of these symptoms usually requires emergency intervention, no matter what the cause.

Bipolar disorder is also known as manic-depressive illness because of the characteristic swings in mood from a hypereuphoric state to a sad and depressed state. These shifts in mood and behavior are often extreme and severe. The manic phase is characterized by a marked increase in energy and a decreased need for sleep. Thoughts may become rapid and racing, called a flight of ideas. The person may have difficulty concentrating and be easily distracted, and he or she may become extremely irritable or angry. Speech may become rapid and pressured, and there may be a significant increase in talking. There may be increases in sex drive and activity or other impulsive and often reckless behaviors, such as spending too much money, driving recklessly, risky sexual behavior, substance abuse, or other behaviors that exhibit poor judgment and low impulse control. There may be a marked increase in goal-directed activity or psychomotor agitation. The person may use substances to enhance the euphoria, or they may try to decrease the irritability and agitation. Manic episodes may be triggered by alcohol and drug use. Stressful events, both positive and negative, can also trigger an episode. Changes in daily schedule sleep patterns and even seasonal changes are also common triggers.

Major depressive episodes are characterized by depressed, sad, or blue moods most of the day. People may lose interest or stop participating in pleasurable activities, and their sex drive may diminish. They may develop sleep disturbance and sleep too much (hypersomnia) or not sleep at all (insomnia). They may experience an increase or decrease in appetite resulting in weight loss or weight gain. This is considered clinically significant if it is greater than +/− 5 percent of total body weight in a month. They may experience restlessness and agitation (psychomotor) or retardation. Fatigue and loss of energy is common as is difficulty concentrating and making decisions. Feelings of worthlessness and guilt may be present as may recurrent thoughts of suicide or death. Clients who show signs of depression should always be continuously assessed for suicide risks. Also, according to the DSM-IV-TR (2000):

> . . . completed suicide occurs in 10%–15% of individuals with Bipolar I Disorder. Suicidal ideation and attempts are more likely to occur when the individual is in a depressive or mixed state. Child abuse, spouse abuse, or other violent behavior may occur during severe manic episodes or during those with psychotic features. (384–85)

The DSM-IV-TR (2000) also states that an "age of onset for a first manic episode after age 50 years should alert the clinician to the possibility that the symptoms may be due to a general medical condition or substance use (360)."

The bipolar client may vacillate between episodes of mania and depression. They may experience what is described as a hypomanic episode that is a lesser version of a full-blown manic episode. Episodes of depression accompanied by episodes of hypomania (but no episodes of full mania) are called Bipolar II Disorder. Symptoms of psychosis (delusions and hallucinations) can accompany either manic or depressive episodes. Often these hallucinations and delusions are considered mood congruent, such as grandiose delusions during manic episodes or delusions of guilt or worthlessness during depressive episodes. Paranoid delusions and other mood-incongruent delusions could be present as well. For the clinician, differentiating major depression from bipolar disorder may be difficult if the client is presenting with symptoms of depression only, unless it can be determined that the client has ever had a manic episode at some time in his or her life. Therefore, specific questioning when assessing the client along these lines should be included (Albanese and Pies, 2004).

Treatment for bipolar disorder may include a combination of medications and psychotherapy. The focus of treatment should be on stabilizing moods, thinking, and behavior, and on symptom relief. Bipolar clients would especially benefit from psychoeducation regarding stress management and the development of positive coping skills. Assessing substance use; teaching clients to avoid alcohol/drugs; and teaching them to utilize relapse prevention skills are important in stabilizing their moods and behavior. It is important for the clinician to note that acute mania symptoms can be mimicked or induced by intoxication with stimulants, hallucinogens, or other polydrug combinations. Also, substance use and discontinuance can be associated with depressive symptoms (CSAT, 2004). Clinicians should be alert to clients in substance abuse treatment settings who present with increased irritability or acting out behaviors as possibly experiencing underlying affective symptoms (Levin and Hennessey, 2004). Studies of effective treatment of co-occurring bipolar disorder and substance use disorders have supported the use of an integrated treatment approach, including the use of relapse prevention treatment that is cognitive-behavioral based.

One specific study used a form of Integrated Group Therapy (IGT) that incorporated treatment strategies for both disorders and stressed the negative impact of substance use on bipolar disorder (Weiss, Najavits, and Greenfield, 1999). Specifically, the IGT approach delineated in this study was a twenty-week structured group process that covered several core components during each session. These included (1) a brief check-in where mood, medication compliance, and substance use during the past week were discussed; (2) a review of the topic from the previous week group session; and (3) a discussion of the topic for the current session. Examples of session topics included "Managing Bipolar Disorder without Abusing Substances," "Denial, Ambivalence, Admitting, and Acceptance," "Taking Medication," "Identification of Triggers for Substance Abuse, Mania, and Depression," "Recognizing Relapse Warning

Signs of Substance Abuse and Mood Disorder Symptoms," and "Self-care." A more recent study by the same author (Weiss, Kolodziej, Griffin, Najavits, Jacobson, and Greenfield, 2004) found that among twenty-one IGT-treated bipolar patients with coexisting substance dependence, those patients who perceived that substance use improved bipolar symptoms (such as racing thoughts or depression) reported fewer days of drug use than non-IGT treated bipolar patients who had the same perception. This suggests that IGT may be effective for this specific subgroup of bipolar-substance abusing clients.

Basic medication strategies for treating co-occurring bipolar-substance abuse will be discussed in a later chapter; however, what is most important for the substance abuse and/or mental health clinician is to reinforce and support medication compliance. Bipolar and other affective disorder clients who comply with their medication regimen are more likely to stabilize and return to a higher level of functioning, including decreased use of drugs and alcohol (Albanese and Pies, 2004).

A recently published study by Drake, Xie, McHugo, and Shumbay (2004) examined three-year outcomes for long-term patients with co-occurring bipolar and substance use disorders. The study followed fifty-one patients with these disorders for three years as they participated in integrated dual disorders treatment. Overall, the patients' psychiatric symptoms improved modestly, but their remission from substance abuse improved steadily. A reported 61 percent of the participants were in full remission at three years. They also achieved greater percentages of independent living, competitive employment, and regular social contacts with nonsubstance abusers. This study supports the notion that long-term patients with disabling co-occurring substance abuse and bipolar disorder can achieve a significant improvement in functioning and quality of life. Engagement of these clients for the long term may also be an important factor in positive outcomes as several of the participants struggled with remission and relapse. This should be taken into consideration as many mental health and substance abuse treatment programs will discontinue/discharge clients who are unable to maintain abstinence and who relapse. Clearly, a more flexible approach and philosophy is indicated for these types of clients.

It is generally accepted that the most effective treatments of affective disorders involve a combination of cognitive-behavioral interventions, illness management, and psychopharmacological interventions. This also appears to be true among those with a co-occurring substance use disorder. A recent study suggests that the patient's ability to self-regulate mood symptoms without using substances is an important component to treatment. The development of alternative coping strategies and strategies to regulate internal discomfort are critical to the patient's success (Myrick et al., 2004).

ANXIETY DISORDERS

Similar to mood disorders, anxiety disorders are prevalent among persons with substance use disorders. The anxiety disorders most prevalent in persons with a substance use disorder are panic disorder, obsessive-compulsive disorder, post-traumatic stress disorder, social phobia, and generalized anxiety disorder (Reiger et al., 1990). The DSM-IV-TR (2000) identifies several subcategories of anxiety disorders, some of which are listed above. Substance use can follow the onset of anxiety symptoms, but can also be the source. We will look at some of the characteristics of these various disorders as they relate to substance use.

Panic disorder refers to recurrent unexpected panic attacks. Panic attacks are defined in the DSM-IV-TR (2000) as:

> . . . a discrete period in which there is the sudden onset of intense apprehension, fearfulness, or terror, often associated with feelings of impending doom. During this attack, symptoms such as shortness of breath, palpitations, chest pain or discomfort, choking or smothering sensations, and fear of going crazy or losing control are present. (429)

When experiencing a panic attack, the person often seeks medical attention or visits an emergency room because they believe they are having a heart attack or some other serious medical problem. Sometimes the person may begin to restrict their behavior by avoiding situations or places that they believe may trigger a panic attack. In some cases, they may become homebound and unwilling to leave because they do not want to experience another panic attack. This is called agoraphobia and may occur with or without a history of panic attacks. Often, the persistent worry and fear of having another panic attack will precipitate another attack. Major depression may co-occur in up to 10 to 65 percent of persons with panic disorder, and there is an approximate prevalence of 35 percent for comorbid substance abuse and panic disorder. It is believed that some individuals may use alcohol or other substances to treat their anxiety symptoms. People with panic disorder, especially those with agoraphobia, may be difficult to engage in treatment because of their unwillingness to leave their home or to travel to appointments or treatment programs.

Social phobia, also known as social anxiety disorder, is characterized by a marked and persistent fear of social or performance situations in which embarrassment may occur (such as public speaking, meeting new people, socializing at parties, or novel social situations). The DSM-IV-TR (2000) states that "exposure to the social or performance situation almost invariably provokes and immediate anxiety response. . . may take the form of a situationally bound panic attack" (450).

The person with social phobia will likely avoid situations which cause distress or if unable to avoid them will participate with a great deal of distress or discomfort. The DSM-IV-TR (2000) describes several commonly associated features such as "hypersensitivity to criticism, negative evaluation, or rejection; difficulty being assertive; and low self-esteem or feelings of inferiority . . . poor social skills; underachievement in school/work" (452).

Individuals with social phobia may withdraw from or isolate themselves from social supports and have difficulties establishing and maintaining friendships and social relationships. Substance use may begin to alleviate the distress and anxiety in these uncomfortable situations (e.g., "a shot of courage") and develop into an abuse/dependency situation as the person becomes reliant on the substance to help them feel more at ease in the social situation.

Obsessive-compulsive disorder is characterized by recurrent, persistent, and intrusive thoughts or images (obsessions) and/or by repetitive or ritualistic behaviors or mental acts that must be performed in order to prevent or reduce anxiety or distress (compulsions). According to the DSM-IV-TR (2000), it is important for the person to recognize that these thoughts and behaviors are excessive, unreasonable, and the product of their own mind. These obsessions and compulsions must cause marked distress, be time-consuming (more than one hour per day), and significantly interfere with the person's normal routine, occupational or social functioning, or relationships. The DSM-IV-TR (2000) also reports that the most common obsessions are:

> . . . repeated thoughts about contamination, repeated doubts (e.g., having left a door unlocked), a need to have things in a particular order (e.g., intense distress when things are disordered or asymmetrical), aggressive or horrific impulses (e.g., to hurt one's child or shout an obscenity in church), and sexual imagery. (457)

The most common compulsions involve repetitive behaviors (such as hand washing, ordering, checking) or mental acts (e.g., praying, counting, repeating words silently) the goal of which is to prevent or reduce anxiety. Excessive use of alcohol, sedative, hypnotic, or anxiolytic medications may be present as individuals attempt to reduce their discomfort or decrease their anxiety levels.

Post-traumatic stress disorder (PTSD) is very prevalent in persons with a co-occurring substance use disorder. More women are diagnosed with this condition than men, although there seems to be an increasing number of men who are experiencing this disorder. For many women (and men), this disorder is the result of childhood trauma from physical and/or sexual abuse. Also, those with substance use disorders and those with serious mental illness are at risk for repeated traumatic experiences related to their substance-using lifestyle (e.g., domestic violence, rape, physical violence, criminal activity, accidents, etc.). Post-traumatic stress disorder can be an acute reaction to a recent traumatic event or delayed for at least six months or longer, following a traumatic event. It is not uncommon for victims of traumatic experiences, especially during childhood, to repress or block out memories of those experiences. Many times these memories and experiences will surface when exposed to further trauma or reminded of the original trauma. The reexperiencing of the traumatic event and the associated feelings are called flashbacks. Sometimes people experiencing these feelings may experience periods of disassociation. These are related to other disorders as well, such as borderline personality disorder and disassociative identity disorder. At least one study has identified that PTSD, borderline personality disorder, and a history of childhood abuse occur with regularity in women receiving substance abuse treatment (Gil-Rivas, Fiorentine, and Anglin, 1996).

The DSM-IV-TR (2000) identifies the following diagnostic criteria for PTSD:

I. The person has experienced, witnessed, or was confronted with an event that involved actual or threatened death or serious injury, or a threat to the physical integrity of self or others.
II. The person's response involved intense fear, helplessness, or horror and the traumatic event is persistently reexperienced in one or more of the following ways:
   A. Recurrent and intrusive distressing recollections of the event, including images, thoughts, or perceptions.
   B. Recurrent distressing dreams of the event.
   C. Acting or feeling as if the traumatic event were recurring (flashbacks, sense of reliving experiences, hallucinations, and disassociation).
   D. Intense psychological distress at exposure to internal or external cues that symbolize or resemble an aspect of the traumatic event.
   E. Physiological reactivity on exposure to internal or external cues that symbolize or resemble an aspect of the traumatic event.
III. Persistent avoidance of stimuli associated with the trauma and numbing of general responsiveness as indicated by three or more of the following:
   A. Efforts to avoid thoughts, feelings, or conversations associated with the trauma.
   B. Efforts to avoid activities, places, or people that arouse recollections of the trauma.
   C. Inability to recall an important aspect of the trauma.
   D. Markedly diminished interest or participation in significant activities.
   E. Feeling of detachment or estrangement from others.

    F. Restricted range of affect (e.g., unable to have loving feelings).

    G. Sense of a foreshortened future (e.g., does not expect to have a career, marriage, children, or a normal life span).

IV. Persistent symptoms of increased arousal (not present before the trauma) as indicated by two or more of the following:

    A. Difficulty falling or staying asleep.

    B. Irritability or outbursts of anger.

    C. Difficulty concentrating.

    D. Hypervigilance.

    E. Exaggerated startle response. (467–68)

These symptoms must persist for at least one month and cause clinically significant impairment in functioning in most life areas. It should be noted that PTSD can co-occur with other mental disorders in addition to substance use disorders. In a study of one hundred treatments seeking cocaine and alcohol abusers, there was a high comorbidity of mental disorders with 48 percent of the men and 70 percent of the women having either an affective or anxiety disorder in addition to other mental disorders (e.g., antisocial personality disorder, obsessive-compulsive disorder). In the study, 46 percent of the women vs. 24 percent of the men were diagnosed with lifetime PTSD (Brady, Grice, Dustan, and Randall, 1993). These findings were supported in a more recent study on the comorbidity of PTSD and other psychiatric disorders conducted by the same author (Brady et al., 2000).

One of the problems often encountered by clinicians who treat clients with a co-occurring substance use disorder and PTSD is that when substance use is discontinued, the PTSD symptoms emerge, sometimes strongly. There is some controversy about whether it is prudent to address trauma issues in early recovery. Some fear that addressing these issues may precipitate anxiety and other feelings that could lead to a relapse of the substance abuse. Others feel that failure to address these issues could set the client up for relapse of substance use to deal with the symptoms of PTSD. Also, for many clinicians, dealing with issues of trauma (often including childhood physical and/or sexual abuse, rape, violence, and other traumas) may be beyond their scope of practice. Given the prevalence of this disorder in clients being treated for substance abuse, all treatment programs should have relationships with clinicians qualified to assess and treat PTSD, as well as other disorders.

Recent studies on the association between smoking and the subsequent onset of panic disorder, agoraphobia, and/or PTSD showed that current smoking was a more powerful predictor of the onset of these disorders. The authors are not sure if this association is due to nicotine dependence or due to lifestyle factors related to trauma exposure leading to a psychological vulnerability that predicts PTSD, once exposed to trauma or to some combination of these processes (Breslau, 2004; Kessler, 2004).

PERSONALITY DISORDERS

The most prevalent personality disorders among people with co-occurring mental illness and substance use disorders are the antisocial and borderline types. In fact, antisocial personality disorder (ASPD) is considered a common factor in persons with both a co-occurring mental illness and substance use disorder (Mueser et al., 2003). Personality disorders are defined as rigid, inflexible, and maladaptive behavior patterns of sufficient severity to cause internal distress or significant impairment in functioning (CSAT, 2004). People with personality disorders carry with them destructive patterns of thinking, feeling, and behaving as their way of interacting with the world. They tend to frame reality in terms of their own needs and perceptions and do not understand the perceptions of others.

Borderline personality disorder (BPD) is characterized by several specific criteria. One essential feature of this disorder is a pervasive pattern of instability in interpersonal relationships along with distortions in self-image and marked impulsivity. People with borderline personality disorder may use drugs in an attempt to decrease inner tension or feelings of losing control. Polydrug use is common, and use patterns are often impulsive and unpredictable. Individuals with BPD are also highly manipulative and may use and abuse multiple medications. They often engage in self-harm (cutting, self-mutilation) and/or suicidal behavior (CSAT, 2004).

The DSM-IV-TR (2000) lists the following as criteria for diagnosing borderline personality disorder:

I. A pervasive pattern of instability of interpersonal relationships, self-image, and affects, and marked impulsivity beginning by early adulthood and present in a variety of contexts as indicated by five (or more) of the following:
   A. Frantic efforts to avoid real or imagined abandonment.
   B. A pattern of unstable and intense interpersonal relationships characterized by alternating between extremes of idealization and devaluation.
   C. Identity disturbance, a markedly and persistently unstable self-image or sense of self.
   D. Impulsivity in at least two areas that are potentially self-damaging (e.g., spending, sex, substance abuse, reckless driving, binge eating).
   E. Recurrent suicidal behavior, gestures, or threats, or self-mutilating behavior.

F. Affective instability due to a marked reactivity of mood (e.g., intense episodic dysphoria, irritability, or anxiety usually lasting a few hours and only rarely more than a few days).
G. Chronic feelings of emptiness.
H. Inappropriate, intense anger or difficulty controlling anger (e.g., frequent displays of temper, constant anger, recurrent physical fights).
I. Transient, stress-related, paranoid ideation or severe disassociative symptoms. (710)

The DSM-IV-TR (APA, 2000) also states that:

Individuals with borderline personality disorder may have a pattern of undermining themselves at the moment a goal is about to be realized (e.g., dropping out of school just before graduation; regressing severely after a discussion of how well therapy is going; destroying a good relationship just when it is clear that the relationship could last). Some individuals develop psychotic-like symptoms (e.g., hallucinations, body-image distortions, ideas of reference, and hypnagogic phenomena) during times of stress. Individuals with this disorder may feel more secure with transitional objects (e.g., a pet or inanimate possession) than in interpersonal relationships. Premature death from suicide may occur in individuals with this disorder, especially in those with co-occurring mood disorders or substance related disorders. Physical handicaps may result from self-inflicted abuse behaviors or failed suicide attempts. Recurrent job losses, interrupted education, and broken marriages are common. Physical and sexual abuse, neglect, hostile conflict, and early parental loss or separation is more common in the childhood histories of those with borderline personality disorder. (708)

Clients with BPD may not do well in traditional substance abuse treatment settings unless the staff is experienced and qualified to treat BPD. Unfortunately, many of these clients will present themselves in mental health and substance abuse treatment settings. Because of their chaotic and dramatic behaviors, they usually present the treatment team with multiple dilemmas. For example, clients with BPD will often create splits between staff or staff and clients. They may create situations that require the clinicians to take action (e.g., suicide threats) and then become angry at the clinician for doing so. They may become angry and/or suicidal at the perceived abandonment by the clinician who is out on vacation. They often present in crisis and will knowingly or unknowingly create crisis situations and demand immediate response from others. When others fail to react or respond to their perceived needs, they will interpret this as rejection or abandonment.

Fortunately, treatment for BPD is available in the form of a cognitive-behavioral based treatment called Dialectical Behavioral Therapy (Linehan,

Schmidt, Dimeff, Craft, Kanter, and Comtois, 1999). This approach is designed to help the client utilize cognitive and harm reduction strategies to manage internal dysregulation and impulsive and destructive behaviors. It has proven quite effective for clients with this disorder, especially in reducing substance abuse in clients with co-occurring substance use disorders.

Some techniques that are helpful for BPD clients with co-occurring disorders are:

- Contracting. This involves clear and direct communication in simple terms (e.g., "If I feel like drinking, I will call my sponsor and go to an AA meeting"; "If I feel like hurting myself, I will call my therapist and/or go to the hospital immediately").
- Counseling. Sessions should concentrate on the development of new skills and the targeting of specific areas where lack of impulse control or self-harm is the focus.
- Boundary setting. This technique with BPD clients is important as is teaching the clients to set and respect healthy boundaries with others.

ANTISOCIAL PERSONALITY DISORDER

As previously stated, antisocial personality disorder (ASPD) is very prevalent in persons with a substance use disorders and especially in those with a co-occurring mental disorder (Mueser et al., 1999).

CSAT (2004) states that:

The two essential features of antisocial personality disorder are (1) a pervasive disregard for and violation of the rights of others and (2) an inability to form meaningful interpersonal relationships.

The prevalence of antisocial personality disorder and substance abuse is high:

- Much of substance abuse treatment is particularly targeted to those with APD, and substance abuse treatment alone has been particularly effective for these disorders.
- The majority of people with substance abuse disorders are not sociopathic except as a result of their addiction.
- Most people diagnosed as having APD are not true psychopaths—that is, predators who use manipulation, intimidation, and violence to control others and to satisfy their own needs.
- Many people with APD use substances in a polydrug pattern involving alcohol, marijuana, heroin, cocaine, and methamphetamine.
- People with APD may be excited by the illegal drug culture and may have considerable pride in their ability to thrive in the face of the dangers of that

culture. They often are in trouble with the law. Those who are more effective may limit themselves to exploitative or manipulative behaviors that do not make them as vulnerable to criminal sanctions. (224–25)

People with ASPD are difficult to engage in treatment and will often enter treatment as a result of legal conditions or consequences. They may come from or be seen in jail or prison settings and will often enter treatment as a condition of parole or probation. There will usually be a history of interactions with the criminal justice system. In this vein, there is leverage in keeping the client in treatment by using a coordinated effort between the criminal justice and treatment systems. People with ASPD are best managed in a strict program that holds clients accountable for their behavior and its resultant consequences (Mueser et al., 1999). Direct confrontation of dishonesty and antisocial behavior and teaching alternative responses is an effective approach with this population.

CSAT (2004) reports that:

It is important to differentiate true antisocial personality from substance-related antisocial behavior. This can best be done by looking at how the person relates to others throughout the course of his or her life. Persons with this disorder will have evidence of antisocial behavior preceding substance use and even during periods of enforced abstinence. It also is important to recognize that people with substance-related antisocial behavior may be more likely to have major depression than other typical personality disorders. (225–26)

The DSM-IV-TR (APA, 2000) delineates the following as criteria for antisocial personality disorder:

I. There is a pervasive pattern of disregard for and violation of the rights of others occurring since age 15, as indicated by three or more of the following:
   A. Failure to conform to social norms with respect to lawful behaviors as indicated by repeatedly performing acts that are grounds for arrest.
   B. Deceitfulness, as indicated by repeated lying, use of aliases, or conning others for personal profit or pleasure.
   C. Impulsivity or failure to plan ahead
   D. Irritability and aggressiveness as indicated by repeated physical fights or assaults.
   E. Reckless disregard for the safety of self or others.
   F. Consistent irresponsibility, as indicated by repeated failure to sustain consistent work behavior or honor financial obligations.
   G. Lack of remorse, as indicated by being indifferent to or rationalizing having hurt, mistreated, or stolen from another. (701–702, 706)

Clients with ASPD can be quite difficult to work with as they are often resistant and manipulative. They do tend to respond to structured treatment that focuses on accountability for one's behavior and the consequences of one's actions. Research has also shown that cognitive-behavioral techniques are effective, especially ones that focus on thinking errors and skill building. One study describes a twenty-four week, manual guided, cognitive-behavioral approach for treating individuals with a co-occurring substance use disorder and ASPD (Ball, 1998).

Chapter Four

Addictive Disorders

SUBSTANCE DEPENDENCE AND ABUSE

The American Psychiatric Association's *Diagnostic and Statistical Manual of Mental Disorders* (DSM-IV-TR) lists the criteria for substance dependence and substance abuse. All clinicians working in either a mental health treatment setting or a substance abuse treatment setting should become familiar with the criteria for a substance use disorder. While assessment for substance use is the norm in substance abuse treatment settings, it is not the case in mental health settings where clinicians frequently fail to assess for substance use/abuse/dependence (Mueser et al., 2003). In a previous chapter on assessment, there was detailed information on doing an alcohol/drug use history.

The following are the criteria for diagnosing substance dependence as outlined in the DSM-IV-TR (2000):

I. A maladaptive pattern of substance use, leading to clinically significant impairment or distress, as manifested by three or more of the following occurring at any time in the same 12-month period:
  A. Tolerance, as defined by either one of the following:
    1. A need for markedly increased amounts of the substance to achieve intoxication or the desired effect.
    2. Markedly diminished effect with continued use of the same amount of the substance.
  B. Withdrawal, as manifested by either of the following:
    1. The characteristic withdrawal syndrome for the substance.
    2. The same (or a closely related) substance is taken to relieve or avoid withdrawal symptoms.

C. The substance is often taken in larger amounts or over a longer period than was intended.

D. There is a persistent desire or unsuccessful efforts to cut down or control substance use.

E. A great deal of time is spent in activities necessary to obtain the substance (e.g., visiting multiple doctors or driving long distances), use the substance (e.g., chain smoking), or recovering from its effects.

F. Important social, occupational, or recreational activities are given up or reduced because of substance use.

G. The substance use is continued despite knowledge of having a persistent or recurrent physical or psychological problem that is likely to have been caused or exacerbated by the substance (e.g., current use despite recognition of cocaine-induced depression, or continued drinking despite recognition that an ulcer was made worse by alcohol consumption).

H The clinician must also specify if there is physiological dependence (evidence of tolerance or withdrawal) or not. (197)

Substance abuse (DSM-IV-TR) is defined by the following criteria:

I. A maladaptive pattern of substance use leading to clinically significant impairment or distress, as manifested by on or more of the following, occurring within a 12-month period:

A. Recurrent substance use resulting in a failure to fulfill major role obligations at work, school, or home (e.g., repeated absences or poor work performance related to substance use; substance related absences, suspensions, or expulsions from school; neglect of children or household).

B. Recurrent substance use in situations in which it is physically hazardous (e.g., driving an automobile or operating a machine when impaired by substance use).

C. Recurrent substance related legal problems (e.g., arrests for substance related disorderly conduct).

D. Continued substance use despite having persistent or recurrent social or interpersonal problems caused or exacerbated by the effects of the substance (e.g., arguments with spouse about consequences of intoxication, physical fights).

In addition to substance use disorders, there are problems related to substance intoxication and withdrawal that mimic or cause psychiatric symptoms. The following are common symptoms that result from the use or withdrawal from specific substances. Clinicians should be aware of these symptoms because clients who present themselves for either mental health treatment or substance abuse treatment can be misdiagnosed and treated. In general, all clients who present for treatment that exhibit psychiatric symptoms regardless of the treatment setting should be assessed for alcohol/drug use. If possible, urine or blood analysis should be conducted in order to ascertain the presence of drugs or alcohol.

Stimulants

Generally, stimulant intoxication will cause an increased physiological response such as elevated blood pressure, increased heart rate, palpitations, perspiration, chills, euphoria, hyperactivity, and pupillary dilation. These symptoms mimic and/or cause symptoms that are consistent with anxiety. In higher doses and longer term use, stimulants can cause grandiose thinking and psychotic symptoms such as delusions (paranoid and grandiose) and hallucinations. Acute intoxication can cause incoherence, loosening of associations, and sometimes tactile hallucinations involving bugs crawling on or under the skin. Heavy stimulant users often have scabs related to picking the skin to remove the "bugs." These psychotic symptoms can mimic and/or be confused with schizophrenia or bipolar disorder. It is not uncommon for these symptoms (e.g., paranoia) to remain for some time following cessation of stimulant use. The symptoms of stimulant withdrawal are generally the opposite of the symptoms of intoxication. Withdrawal symptoms usually include fatigue, dysphoric mood, depression, insomnia or hypersomnia, irritability, emotional lability, and increased appetite. According to the DSM-IV-TR (APA, 2000) there is often a "crash" following a high dose speed "run." The depressed symptoms may include suicidal ideation. Strong cravings to use the drug may be present. The clinician should be careful to assess risk factors often present due to the depression and possible suicidal ideation that may increase as discomfort increases.

Depressants

This category includes alcohol, benzodiazepines, barbiturates, and other sedative type drugs. In general, substance intoxication involves increasing psychological and physiological changes, such as impaired judgment and impulse control, mood changes, slurred speech, coordination and mobility problems, stupor or coma, and depression of CNS (central nervous system) functions (breathing, heart rate, etc.). Alcohol use causes relaxation, sedation, and reduced inhibitions in addition to the above listed effects. Withdrawal from alcohol can be serious and even life-threatening depending on the amount and length of time a person has used alcohol.

The DSM-IV-TR (APA, 2000) describes the following criteria for alcohol withdrawal:

I. Cessation of or reduction in alcohol use that has been heavy and prolonged.
II. Two or more of the following, developing within several hours to a few days after Criterion I:
    A. Autonomic hyperactivity (e.g., sweating or pulse rate greater than 100).
    B. Increased hand tremor.
    C. Insomnia.
    D. Nausea or vomiting.
    E. Transient visual, tactile, or auditory hallucinations or illusions.
    F. Psychomotor agitation.
    G. Anxiety.
    H. Grand mal seizures.
III. The symptoms in Criterion II cause clinically significant distress or impairment in social, occupational, or other important areas of functioning. (216)

Some individuals may experience a condition known as alcohol withdrawal delirium, also known as delirium tremens or "DTs." This includes disturbances in consciousness, cognition, visual, auditory, and tactile hallucinations. Delirium tremens is a serious medical condition and requires immediate medical intervention. Persons experiencing this condition may present as psychotic and be mistakenly diagnosed as having an acute mental illness; therefore, clinicians should familiarize themselves with procedures for identifying and managing clients with this condition.

Sedative, hypnotic, and anxiolytic drugs are typically prescription medications taken for anxiety or insomnia that have a high potential for abuse and dependency. These include medications such as the benzodiazepines, barbiturates, and sleep aids. Intoxication and withdrawal from these drugs is characterized by symptoms similar to those associated with alcohol. Psychosis is not uncommon and may include hallucinations and delusions as part of the withdrawal delirium. The onset of withdrawal symptoms following cessation of use may be prolonged depending on the specific drug used as some have longer acting properties. Also, the withdrawal symptoms may be experienced over a much longer period of time than alcohol, sometimes over several months. Ironically, individuals who have taken these drugs for a long period of time may develop a dependency on them without taking them in an abusive manner. Often, they (and/or their physician) may confuse the symptoms of withdrawal as a return of the anxiety or insomnia that the drugs are designed to treat, and they are reinstated with the patient/physician believing that they are treating an anxiety disorder or sleep disorder. This situation is often seen in older adults who have been treated with these medications for long periods. The symptoms may be exacerbated and potentiated when combined with alcohol use (Jaffe, 1980).

Marijuana (Cannabis)

Marijuana can cause altered perceptions and act as a mild hallucinogen. Users report hallucinations, paranoid or grandiose delusions, and anxiety-related symptoms, as well. Chronic and heavy marijuana use can also impair thinking, memory, and motivation. These effects can last for some time even after cessation of use. Most commonly, there is an increased sense of well-being or euphoria accompanied by feelings of relaxation and sleepiness (Perkinson, 2002). Physical signs of use include red eyes, strong odor, dilated pupils, and increased pulse rate. With higher doses, short-term memory is impaired, and there is difficulty in carrying out multiple mental tasks. Motor skills and reaction times become impaired. Tolerance can develop with continued use. Withdrawal-like symptoms following cessation of heavy and chronic use of marijuana can include headache, irritability, restlessness, nervousness, decreased appetite, weight loss, and insomnia. Tremor and increased body temperature may occur (Gold, 1994). While withdrawal from cannabis is generally not severe, persons may experience what appear to be depression and anxiety symptoms. These symptoms may be confused for mental disorders. Since the THC (the active ingredient in marijuana) can remain in the body for as long as one month following chronic use, clinicians should monitor clients for possible co-occurring disorders if depressive, anxiety, or other symptoms persist or worsen.

Hallucinogens

This class of drugs includes those that produce marked changes and distortions in perception, behavior, and thinking. By definition, they cause hallucinations, disorientation, and psychosis. Drugs in this group include LSD, PCP, peyote, mescaline, MDMA, and mushrooms. In fact, this class of drugs causes the user to experience significant impairments and psychological changes. There is some evidence that this class of drugs may exacerbate schizophrenic symptoms in persons predisposed to this disorder (APA, 2000). Because of the presence of psychotic symptoms, it may be difficult for the clinician to differentiate between substance-induced symptoms vs. a mental illness. Generally, the effects of the drug begin to wear off after a few hours. Psychotic or anxiety symptoms that persist beyond a few hours are more likely the result of an underlying mental illness and not a result of the substance use.

According to the DSM-IV-TR (APA, 2000):

> Hallucinogen intoxication begins with some stimulant effects such as restlessness and autonomic activation. Nausea may occur. Feelings of euphoria may alternate rapidly with depression or anxiety. Initial visual illusions may give way to hallucinations . . . which are more visual, often of geometric forms or figures, sometimes of persons or objects. In most cases reality testing is preserved (i.e., the person knows the effects are substance induced). (252–53)

Additional symptoms such as paranoia and ideas of reference are also possible. Judgment is impaired as well. Physical symptoms that occur shortly after use can include papillary dilation, tachycardia, sweating, palpitations, blurred vision, tremors, and incoordination. Sometimes a person who uses hallucinogens may reexperience perceptual distortion, similar to those experienced during previous hallucinogen intoxications. These episodes are termed "flashbacks" and are part of a disorder called hallucinogen persisting perception disorder. They may occur episodically and may be self-induced or triggered by entry into a dark environment, ingestion of various drugs, anxiety, fatigue, or other stressors (APA, 2000). They usually go away after a few months but can last longer. These types of flashbacks are more visual-perceptual distortions vs. the ones experienced by persons with PTSD, which are re-creations of the traumatic event.

Certain hallucinogens (PCP) can cause increased aggressive and violent behavior. Because of the psychosis that accompanies hallucinogen use, clients should be kept in a safe setting to avoid harm to self or others. Some intoxicated users have completed suicide by jumping out of windows believing that they could fly.

Opiates

This class of drugs includes heroin, morphine, opium, codeine, and a host of medications used for pain control (analgesics) such as demerol, dilaudid, vicodin, and many others. These drugs cause euphoria, pain relief, sedation, and impairments in attention and memory. Depending on the route of administration, users can experience a warm flushing of the skin and an intense sensation know as the "kick" or "rush" that is described by users as similar to an orgasm (Jaffe, 1980). Opiates are highly addictive, and users quickly develop dependence. Intoxication is characterized by euphoria followed by apathy, dysphoria, psychomotor retardation or agitation, impaired judgment, papillary constriction, drowsiness or coma, slurred speech, and impairments in memory or attention (APA, 2000). Withdrawal symptoms are intense but are not considered life-threatening. Mild withdrawal presents as flu-like symptoms including anxiety, yawning, dysphoria, sweating, runny nose, tearing, papillary dilation, goose bumps, and autonomic nervous system arousal. Severe symptoms include hot and cold flashes, deep muscle and joint pain, nausea, vomiting, diarrhea, abdominal pain, and fever (Perkinson, 2000). Intense cravings and a desire to avoid withdrawal symptoms are deterrents for a person's maintaining abstinence. Depression, anxiety, insomnia, and criminal behavior are associated with opiate dependency. There is also a higher incidence of PTSD (APA, 2000).

Chapter Five

Psychotherapeutic Medications

The use of psychotherapeutic medications in the treatment of severe mental illness (schizophrenia, affective disorders, and anxiety disorders) has been proven effective and necessary. It is the mainstay of treatment (Mueser et al., 2003) for individuals with these disorders. Medication combined with psychotherapy and other forms of psychosocial treatment has yielded the best outcomes for clients with these types of disorders. Clinicians who work in mental health settings have been accustomed to and accepting of the concept of psychotherapeutic medications; however, clinicians in the substance abuse treatment system have been less accepting and knowledgeable of medications and their uses. Much of this stems from a lack of education and training about the various types of medications. For example, there seems to be a widely held belief in the substance abuse treatment and 12-step recovery communities that psychotropic medications are all addictive and that any individual who is on any of these medications is not really clean and sober. Consequently, persons with co-occurring mental disorders may not feel accepted in these communities or may get mixed messages about medications leading to medication noncompliance. While some classes of medications may be contraindicated for persons with a substance use disorder, most psychotherapeutic medications do not have an abuse or dependency potential and are necessary to stabilize and/or eliminate psychiatric symptoms and behaviors. Given the high prevalence of co-occurring mental disorders in persons with substance use disorders, it is clearly necessary for clinicians to become familiar with psychotherapeutic medications and their use in treatment. A primary obstacle has been the lack of available resources in many substance abuse treatment programs. One study of over 175 representative specialty substance abuse treatment programs found that fewer than 54 percent of these programs had even a part-time physician on staff (they did not specify if these were psychiatrists or physicians with any specialized training in addiction medicine) and fewer than 15 percent had a nurse on staff. Social workers and psychologists were rarely mentioned (McLellan and Meyers, 2004).

Psychopharmacology has two major roles in the treatment of dual disorders (Mueser et al., 2003):

1. Stabilization of major mental illness symptoms.
2. Medications specific to the treatment of addiction or with evidence of potential for reducing cravings for substances should be considered.

Medication compliance has been an ongoing problem for persons with severe mental illness. This situation seems to be even more prominent among those with co-occurring substance use disorders. Factors that complicate the noncompliance with medications are those clients with dual disorders who are often warned that their medications may interact dangerously with their use of alcohol and drugs or they may find that their medications can interfere with the "high" they experience from their substance use (Mueser et al., 2003).

Individuals with co-occurring disorders who enter treatment through either system must be assured of getting adequate assessment and treatment. As a rule of thumb, clients who present with severe psychiatric symptoms (psychosis, mania, depression, anxiety, and delirium) should have those symptoms treated and stabilized, even if they are caused by the abused substance. While substance-induced symptoms usually remit within several days of stopping substance use, it is recommended that pharmacological treatment not be withheld because the client will not be able to engage in or benefit from other psychosocial treatment until stabilized.

The following is a summary of the various classes of psychotherapeutic medications and their uses. Clinicians are encouraged to develop their knowledge and familiarity with these medications.

ANTIPSYCHOTICS

These medications are primarily used to treat the symptoms of schizophrenia and mania. They are designed to eliminate or reduce the psychotic symptoms (hallucinations and delusions) that may be present in persons with schizophrenia (or other psychotic disorder), bipolar disorder, or severe depression. They may also be used to treat psychotic symptoms induced by substances or by a medical condition. They may also help improve or slow down disorganized thinking and negative symptoms. These medications fall into two primary classes, atypical and traditional. The atypicals are newer medications that are reported to have fewer unpleasant side effects and may help to improve medication compliance. The traditionals are the older medications that are effective and sometimes combined with the atypicals to produce the desired outcome. They often have unpleasant and sometimes dangerous side effects such as extrapyramidal symptoms (tremor, restlessness, agitation, muscle stiffness, and other Parkinsonian symptoms) and a condition know as Tardive Dyskenisia (involuntary movements of mouth and tongue, jerky movements of limbs or body) that is a neurological condition that may be permanent. While atypicals and traditionals can both have these side effects, they are more prevalent in the older medications. Clients who have difficulties with medication compliance may benefit from certain forms of these medications that come in the form of long-acting injectables (Haldol, Prolixin, and Resperidal Consta). The following table is a partial list of these medications.

Table 5.1. Antipsychotic Medications

Atypical Antipsychotics	Traditional Antipsychotics
Abilify	Thorazine
Clozaril	Prolixin
Zyprexa	Haldol
Serouqel	Mellaril
Resperidal	Navane
Geodon	Stelazine

While these medications are all effective in treating the above listed symptoms, some may have special applications in the treatment of co-occurring substance use disorders. For example, the use of Clozaril has been found to improve substance abuse outcomes in schizophrenic patients as compared to those patients on other antipsychotic medications (Xie et al., in press; Drake, Xie, McHugo, and Green, 2000). Unfortunately, this medication must be monitored closely with regular blood tests due to a serious side effect called agranulocytosis, a critical blood disorder (Mueser and McGurk, 2004). The medication Zyprexa has been shown to reduce substance abuse and craving in schizophrenic patients (Conley, Kelly, and Gale, 1998).

In addition to treatment for schizophrenia, the atypical antipsychotics have also been effective in the treatment of mania in clients with bipolar disorder. Usually these medications are combined with other antimanic medications (listed in table 5.2), although they can be used alone with favorable results in some patients.

ANTIMANICS

These drugs are used to control the mood swings of bipolar disorder. Usually, individuals with this disorder experience severe and/or frequent changes from extreme highs to extreme lows. The extremes may vary in terms of frequency and intensity. Severe depression, if untreated, may be incapacitating and could lead to suicidal thinking and behavior. Severe mania can lead to several problems including psychosis. Antimanic medications help to level out the mood swings and keep them from reaching either extreme. Table 5.2 is a partial list of these medications.

Table 5.2. Antimanic Medications

Antimanics	*Anticonvulsants*
Lithium (Eskalith, Lithobid)	Tegretol
	Depakote
	Neurontin
	Lamictal
	Trileptal
	Topamax
	Gabatril

Lithium is considered the gold standard of treatment for bipolar disorder. Because the therapeutic level and the toxic level are so close and because individuals on this medication can vary in their ability to tolerate the side effects, regular blood level monitoring is required. Myrick et al. (2004) report that there are several studies describing a suboptimal response to lithium in comorbid patients.

One article reviewed several studies that looked at certain medications used on substance abusers with bipolar (or bipolar spectrum) disorders (Levin and Hennesy, 2004). The studies considered lithium, anticonvulsants, and quetiapine (Seroquel). They reported that mood symptomatology improved regardless of the medication used or the substance abused by the patients. It was unclear if drug or alcohol use diminished or not. Levin and Hennesy report that some studies have shown dually diagnosed patients were more likely to comply with valproate (Depakote) than lithium, possibly because of fewer side effects (Weiss et al., 2004). They also report that patients who received an anticonvulsant, alone or in combination with lithium, were more likely to have a remission of symptoms than those treated with lithium alone. The authors site one study (Brady, Sonne, Malcolm, Randall, Simpson, Dansky, et al., 2002) evaluating cocaine-dependent clients with comorbid histories of affective disorders. The study reports a trend for the cabamazepine (Tegretol) group with affective disorders to have fewer positive cocaine drug tests than the placebo group. Albanese and Pies (2004) suggest that the strategy of combining lithium with an anticonvulsant may be indicated in bipolar substance-abusing patients due to the antisuicide properties associated with lithium and the higher risk of suicide in this population. Ballasiotes and Skaer (2000) report the use of lamotrigine (Lamictal) in a patient with comorbid substance use disorders, and bipolar disorder resulted in stabilization of the patient's mood and remission of substance abuse. Albanese and Pies (2004) also reviewed some studies on the use of topiramate (Topamax) in the treatment of alcoholics (but not with bipolar disorder) and found that these patients experienced a decrease in alcohol intake.

In general, it appears that the most effective pharmacological treatment for treating bipolar disorder (with or without co-occurring substance abuse) is still lithium, alone or in conjunction with anticonvulsants and/or atypical antipsychotics.

ANTIDEPRESSANTS

As the title of this category indicates, the drugs in this class are used for the treatment of depression. Some have uses for other disorders or symptoms as well. There are three primary classes of antidepressant medications. There are the SSRIs (Selective Serotonin Reuptake Inhibitors), non-SSRIs, and tricyclics (TCAs). Another class called Monoamine Oxidase Inhibitors (MAOIs) is also used for treatment of depression but is not indicated for clients with dual disorders due to their potential side effects when certain foods or alcohol is consumed. Most people who are given antidepressants must be on them for at least three to four weeks to achieve the maximum effects in reducing depression. Continuing treatment for depression with medication for at least two years before discontinuing use is recommended. This is because discontinuing antidepressant treatment before the depression is resolved may result in the client becoming medication resistant. The most frequently used medications are the SSRIs, due to their effectiveness and low incidence of unpleasant side effects.

Table 5.3.   Antidepressants

SSRIs	Non-SSRIs	Tricyclics
Celexa	Effexor	Elavil
Lexapro	Wellbutrin	Anafranil
Prozac	Remeron	Sinequan
Paxil	Serzone	Tofranil
Zoloft	Desyrel	Pamelor
		Norpramine

Research on the treatment of co-occurring depression and alcohol dependence has focused on the use of both tricyclics and SSRIs. Pettinati (2004) did a review of such research, and he found studies that supported the use of desipramine (Norpramine) for reducing both depressive symptoms and drinking in alcoholics with comorbid depression. Another study using imipramine (Tofranil) found decreased depression, but little change in drinking. Nonetheless, it is felt that TCAs are moderately beneficial in treating comorbid alcoholism and depression (Myrick et al., 2004). It was noted that higher daily doses of medication may be necessary for alcoholics to achieve the desired effects. This may be a problem in that TCAs can be toxic when combined with alcohol and drugs, so clients in early recovery who are at the highest risk of relapse or clients who are still using substances should not be given these medications (Ries and Consensus Panel, 1994). Relative to SSRIs, there were several studies reviewed by Pettinati (2004). To summarize, these studies looked at the use of fluoxetine (Prozac), setraline (Zoloft), and nefazodone (Serzone), respectively, in patients with comorbid alcoholism and depression. All of the studies cited showed improvements in depression. The fluoxetine and nefazodone studies showed a reduction in alcohol use as well. Pettinati points out that these studies are inconsistent in their results of the effects of fluoxetine on reducing drinking. He suggests that future studies might look at combinations of two medications; one for treating alcohol dependence and one for treating depression. One study of this type cited by the author showed positive results in decreasing both drinking and depression when naltrexone was combined with an SSRI (Salloum, Cornelius, Thase, Daley, Kirisci, and Spotts, 1998).

A recent meta-analytical study reviewing thirty years of literature on the treatment of depression with persons that have concurrent substance abuse problems concluded that treating the depression of patients with co-occurring substance abuse has a moderate benefit. Patients who responded to the antidepressant treatment also showed a reduction of substance use; however, cessation rates were generally low. The authors suggest treatment of the depression with an evidence-based psychosocial treatment followed by antidepressant medication only if the depression does not improve (Nunes and Levin, 2004).

ANTIANXIETY MEDICATIONS

The use of certain antianxiety medications for the treatment of anxiety disorders in persons with a co-occurring substance use disorder is generally contraindicated due to these medications having a strong potential for abuse and dependency. The medications used to treat anxiety are the benzodiazepines, beta-blockers, and others (including some antidepressants, antihistamines, and antipsychotics). The benzodiazepines are the class of medications that have the highest potential for abuse and dependency even in persons without a history of substance abuse. In general, antianxiety medications are used to help decrease the uncomfortable symptoms associated with anxiety and anxiety-related disorders. Because the benzodiazepines are psychoactive and mood altering, they are often used as drugs of abuse. They may be used in conjunction with antipsychotics during the treatment of acute mania or psychosis. They are also used in the management of acute withdrawal from alcohol and sedative-hypnotics. Use beyond these acute stages in patients with dual disorders is not indicated as they may compromise recovery from addiction (Zweben and Smith, 1989). Benzodiazepines are designed to be used for a short period of time. Use for longer than four to eight weeks will cause an increase in physical tolerance. When discontinuing these medications, the client will have to be tapered off slowly to avoid withdrawal symptoms. Abrupt withdrawal after regular use of benzodiazepines may be a life-threatening situation similar to alcohol withdrawal. Also, excessive respiratory depression and sedation may occur in patients who are taking benzodiazepines and clozapine (Clozaril) (Mueser et al., 2003).

Table 5.4. Antianxiety Medicines

Benzodiazepines	Antihistamines	Beta-Blockers	Other
Xanax	Atarax	Inderal	BuSpar
Librium	Vistaril		
Klonopin	Benadryl		
Valium			
Ativan			
Tranxene			
Serax			

Beta-blockers work on the central nervous system and reduce anxiety, especially in people with panic attacks. They are not considered addictive. BuSpar is a nonaddictive medication that reportedly diminishes anxiety symptoms without the mood altering effects of benzodiazepines. It generally takes three to four weeks to achieve maximum effect (Ries and Consensus Panel, 1994). The antihistamines are used because they cause mild sedation and drowsiness which are effective in reducing anxiety. They are not considered to be addictive. The use of SSRI antidepressants may also yield positive results in managing anxiety in some people and should be considered. The dosages may have to be in the upper therapeutic ranges to achieve the desired effects (Mueser et al., 2003).

STIMULANT MEDICATIONS

Drugs in this class are used primarily in the treatment of attention deficit hyperactivity disorder (ADHD) in children and adults. Obviously, there is significant controversy about their use in clients with co-occurring substance use problems. The potential for abuse and dependence is high, although when given in therapeutic dosages, there do not appear to be a high incidence of abuse or dependence. When people with ADHD take stimulant medication at the prescribed dosage, they usually will report feeling normal and will experience an increased ability to concentrate. Some report feeling calmer, and in some cases may experience sedation if overmedicated. This effect occurs most often in children and is known as a paradoxical effect.

There has always been an association between ADHD and substance abuse. It was believed by many that the use of stimulant medications might cause or at least exacerbate substance use and abuse. A recent study showed that individuals with ADHD treated with stimulant medications were actually less likely to become substance abusers (Wilens, Faraone, Biedirman, and Gunawardine, 2003). It may be that untreated ADHD can cause substance use/abuse, possibly as a means of self-medication or some other unknown component of the disorder. Another possible explanation is the association between ADHD and antisocial personality disorder and the prevalence of ASPD among substance abusers and those with other comorbid conditions.

Recently, there have been some new medications that have been used to treat ADHD. Straterra is a nonstimulant medication that works on the epinephrine levels in the brain. This helps increase attention span and decrease hyperactivity in those with ADHD. The antidepressant Wellbutrin has also been used successfully for ADHD and is not a stimulant. Given the high potential for misuse of stimulants, especially in persons with a substance abuse history, they should not be the primary choice for treatment of ADHD symptoms for this population.

Table 5.5. Stimulant and Non-Stimulant Medications

Stimulants	*Non-Stimulants*
Dexadrine	Strattera
Adderall	Wellbutrin
Ritalin	Cylert
Desoxyn	
Concerta	
Metadate	

MEDICATIONS FOR SUBSTANCE USE DISORDERS

There are a handful of medications that have been used or approved for use in the treatment of substance abuse. Mueser et al. (2003) caution that none of these medications have been studied for their efficacy on clients with co-occurring disorders. Probably the oldest and most widely used medications are disulfiram (Antabuse) and methadone hydrochloride (Methadone). Antabuse is used to treat alcohol abuse/dependence by producing a noxious physical reaction when combined with alcohol. It is designed to be used as an aversive deterrent to alcohol. The client is aware that any alcohol use (even in hygiene products) will produce a violent physical reaction including nausea, vomiting, flushing, headache, sweating, rapid heart rate, blurred vision, and a host of other symptoms. The drug works by inhibiting the metabolism of alcohol, causing acetaldehyde (a by-product of alcohol metabolism that produces the hangover symptoms) to accumulate, causing the severe reaction above. In order for disulfiram to be effective, it must be administered two to five days per week under direct supervision, ideally by a clinician or reliable family members (Brewer, 1992). Disulfiram is intended to create a barrier to drinking for a period of time allowing the client to maintain sobriety. Disulfiram use in clients with dual disorders is considered safe and effective, despite some controversy and concern over use with actively psychotic patients (Mueser et al., 2003). One study of clients with alcoholism and severe mental illness (70 percent with schizophrenia or schizoaffective disorder), treated for an average of two years and followed up for three years, found that 64 percent achieved a remission of their alcoholism for at least one year and 30 percent achieved a remission for at least two to three years (Mueser, Noordsy, Fox, and Wolfe, 2000). The authors point out that clients are asked to report any alcohol use. If reactions are reported after alcohol use, clients are given an emergency medical evaluation. They also suggest that once the alcoholism has been in remission for one to two years, ongoing disulfiram treatment may not be necessary (Mueser et al., 2003).

Methadone has been used in the United States for maintenance treatment of opiate addiction since the 1960s. It is a synthetic, long-acting drug used in heroin and other opiate addiction treatment. When used in proper (monitored) doses, methadone stops the cravings for opiates without any euphoria, sedation, or analgesic effects. Usually persons who wish to stop using heroin or other opiates will go to specialized clinics or programs licensed to dispense this medication. Generally, clients must return to the clinic on a daily (or as required) basis to receive the drug, and they are monitored closely and tested for the presence of other drugs. Participants are usually required to be drug free in order to receive the methadone. Other psychosocial rehabilitation is usually offered and available, but many programs do not require participation in order to receive the drug. Mueser et al. (2003) report that the use of methadone in combination with integrated treatment for dual disorders appears to be a reasonable treatment approach for some clients.

A newer medication for opiate withdrawal or substitution was approved for use in 2002. The medication is called buprenorphine (Suboxone, Subutex) and is approved for use by doctors who have been certified to prescribe, in their offices, instead of licensed clinics with methadone. It is similar to methadone in its ability to suppress opiate withdrawal without the euphoria or rush associated with other opiates. In high doses it may precipitate withdrawal. Sometimes, the two are given together to reduce the risk for buprenorphine abuse by injection. As compared to methadone, buprenorphine is long acting, safe, and effective (Keltner and Folks, 2005). Another drug, clonidine, is also being used to treat acute opioid withdrawal. It suppresses nausea, vomiting, diarrhea, cramps, and sweating, but not muscle aches and insomnia. Keltner and Folks (2005) report that administering naltrexone combined with clonidine can speed withdrawal and lessen withdrawal symptoms from opioids.

Naltrexone (ReVia) is used in the treatment of alcoholism and opiate addiction (Salloum et al., 1998). It completely blocks the pleasurable reinforcement that comes with use of opiates. It also is used to reduce the craving for alcohol and the duration of any relapse of drinking. Mueser et al. (2003) report that it is safe to use with dual disordered clients to help reduce alcohol cravings. It is also useful in reducing alcohol or opiate use if done under proper supervision. Keltner and Folks (2005) report that naltrexone is effective in preventing relapse in alcoholics, especially when combined with psychosocial treatments. Another medication used to reduce cravings for alcohol and decreasing the incidence of relapse is called acamprosate (Campral) (Sass, Soyka, Mann, and Zieglgansberger, 1996).

Table 5.6.   Medications for Substance Abuse Disorders

Addiction Treatment Medications
Antabuse
ReVia
Methadone
Suboxone
Subutex
Campral

Chapter Six

Treatment of Co-occurring Disorders

The treatment of co-occurring disorders must vary from the approaches taken in traditional mental health and substance abuse settings. As previously mentioned, the philosophy of each of these systems is deficient in assessing and treating clients with co-occurring disorders. The confrontational approach used in most traditional substance abuse treatment programs has been shown to be contraindicated with dual disordered clients. Therefore a more client-centered approach may be necessary to engage and retain dual disordered clients in treatment. The requirement of immediate and total abstinence from substances may also keep clients with co-occurring disorders from entering or staying in treatment. While abstinence is recommended as a goal, it is also suggested that programs be flexible and develop individualized treatment plans for each client relative to attaining this goal. Harm reduction strategies can be utilized with clients in the early stages of treatment that may not be ready to make a commitment for change. Interventions should be tailored to the client's readiness to change and the stage of change that they are in. Mental health programs must be more aware of substance use/abuse and become more vigilant in assessing substance use disorders. Treatment of co-occurring disorders must become integrated (treating both disorders simultaneously within the same program or setting), and clinicians should be cross-trained to assess and treat clients with both mental illness and substance use disorders. Clinicians should become familiar with and skilled in evidence-based treatments for co-occurring disorders. The following treatments are necessary ingredients in effective treatment programs for this population.

MOTIVATIONAL INTERVIEWING

Numerous studies have shown that the use of motivational interviewing (MI) techniques with individuals that have co-occurring mental illness and substance abuse produces positive treatment outcomes (Drake et al., 2004; Goldsmith and Garlapati, 2004; Graeber, Moyers, Griffith, Guajardo, and Tonigan, 2003; Carey et al., 2002; Barrowclough et al., 2001; Drake et al., 2001; Bellack and Gearon, 1998; Ziedonis and Trudeau, 1997).

Carroll (2004) reports that motivational approaches are designed to produce rapid (internally motivated) change in substance use and problem behaviors. Drake et al. (2001) found that most dual diagnosis clients have little readiness for abstinence-oriented treatment and many lack the motivation to manage psychiatric illness and pursue employment or other goals. Effective programs incorporate motivational interventions that are designed to help clients become ready for change or open to accepting other types of intervention. Goldsmith and Garlapati (2004) state that motivational interventions are recognized as basic, effective ingredients to addiction treatment, especially when matched with the patient's stages of change (Prochaska and DiClemente, 1984).

Drake et al. (2004) did a comprehensive review of treatments for people with co-occurring mental illness and substance abuse disorders. They reported that treatment outcomes, such as increased engagement in treatment, decreased substance abuse, and increased readiness for more definitive interventions was found in clients who received some form of motivational counseling, either before or concurrent with other forms of intervention.

Motivational interviewing is a technique developed by Miller and Rollnick (2002) to address ambivalence and resistance in clients with substance abuse problems. It was instituted because many of these clients did not respond to traditional methods of confrontation common to substance abuse treatment. In the face of confrontation, many clients would become resistant to change and, in some cases, work in opposition to change, especially if they were ambivalent about change in the first place. The prominent philosophy of the substance abuse treatment field has been that a person must hit bottom in order to be ready for change. Unfortunately for many, bottom was after they had lost everything or reached a point of mental and physical deterioration that was impossible to overcome. People who were resistant and/or ambivalent to change were labeled as in denial or not ready. While denial is certainly an issue with both substance use disorders and mental illness, it is now believed that much of what is called denial may be resistance or ambivalence. It is this ambivalence that must be resolved before change can occur.

Motivational interviewing is defined by Miller and Rollnic[client centered directive method for enhancing intrinsic motiv: by exploring and resolving ambivalence" (25).

Miller and Rollnick (2002) believe that the relationship between the client and the clinician is more important than the technique or method utilized. They also believe that in utilizing a Rogerian client-centered approach, which emphasizes accurate empathy involving skillful reflective listening that clarifies and amplifies the person's own experiencing and meaning, without imposing the counselor's own material (Rogers, 1951). This approach is in direct contrast to the more confrontational style utilized in most traditional substance abuse treatment programs. The authors cite a study by Handmaker, Miller, and Manicke (1999) that showed the more the counselor confronted the client during treatment, the more the client drank within the year following treatment.

Miller and Rollnick (2002) believe that factors active in the early phases of the counseling relationship are most important in facilitating behavioral change. If the client and the counselor both believe that change is possible, the client is more likely to do so. The authors have found that just a few sessions with a counselor under certain specific conditions produces significant results in reducing heavy or problematic drinking. When a clinician pressures a client to change, they actually push a client to become more aware of their ambivalence (Mueser et al., 2003). This increases the client's resistance to change. Thus, in many ways, the client may paradoxically resist change when pressured to do so by the clinician, rather than move toward it.

Miller and Rollnick (2002) describe four general principles that underlie motivational interviewing:

- Express empathy
- Develop discrepancy
- Roll with resistance
- Support self-efficacy

Mueser et al. (2003) add a fifth principle of establishing personal goals for use with clients who have co-occurring disorders. They believe that this is necessary because it requires considerable time, effort, and clinical skill in clients with dual disorders.

Miller and Rollnick (2002) report that acceptance facilitates change. A client-centered and empathic counseling style is a fundamental and defining characteristic of motivational interviewing. They see ambivalence as normal. They state that "the crucial attitude is a respectful listening to the person with a desire to understand his or her perspectives" (37).

In developing discrepancy, the client rather than the counselor should present the arguments for change. Change is motivated by a perceived discrepancy between present behavior and important personal goals or values. MI is directed toward the resolution of ambivalence in the service of change. The clinician should attempt to amplify and increase the discrepancy so that it overrides the tendency to stay where one is instead of changing.

Rolling with the resistance refers to the clinician's avoidance of arguing with the client for change and nonopposition of any resistance that the client may present. The client, not the counselor, is the primary resource for finding answers and solutions, and resistance is a signal to the counselor to respond differently. Failure to do so may increase resistance and cause the client to oppose change rather than move toward it.

Supporting self-efficacy (the person's belief in their ability to carry out and succeed with a specific task) is important for both the client and the counselor. The client must believe that they can successfully change, and the counselor must believe that the client can change as well.

Mueser et al. (2003) suggest that clinicians help to develop dissonance between the client's personal goals and substance use through the development of meaningful and personal goals that are important to the client. Clients with serious mental illness often need support in breaking out of their self-protective shells by increasing self-efficacy.

Miller and Rollnick (2002) discuss the importance of facilitating "change talk" which moves a person toward change vs. resistance that moves the person away from change. They suggest that the counselor can avoid increasing the client's resistance through advocacy responses such as:

- Arguing for change (e.g., trying to persuade client to make changes)
- Assuming the expert role (e.g., lecturing, having all the answers)
- Criticizing, shaming, or blaming (e.g., instilling negative emotions)
- Labeling (e.g., proposing acceptance of a label, diagnosis, and problem)
- Being in a hurry (e.g., getting ahead of the client's readiness)
- Claiming preeminence (e.g., "I know what is best for you"). (50)

Instead they recommend that the clinician work with the client to evoke change talk. They suggest that using open-ended questions in the four following categories is effective in doing this:

- Disadvantages of the status quo (e.g., What do you think will happen if you don't change anything?)
- Advantages of change (e.g., What would be the advantages of making this change?)

- Optimism about change (e.g., What makes you think that if you did decide to make this change that you could do it?)
- Intention to change (e.g., What do you intend to do?)

Miller and Rollnick (2002) summarize the process of motivational interviewing through the acronym OARS that stands for:

1. Ask open-ended questions.
2. Affirm and reinforce change talk.
3. Reflect back change talk.
4. Summarize change talk that the client has elicited.

In short, motivational interviewing is an approach for helping clients to explore the advantages and disadvantages of changing a particular behavior. Many people, especially those with co-occurring disorders, do not always see the negative consequences or impact of their behaviors on themselves and others. They may not understand that change is necessary or know how to make necessary changes. It would not be effective to begin psychoeducation with a client who has not yet accepted or identified the need to change. One may try to persuade clients to change by telling them all of the negative consequences and potential outcomes of their behavior, which may only serve to increase their resistance. Thus, meeting clients at their level of understanding is important in engaging them in the change process.

The process of motivational interviewing is closely tied to the Transtheoretical Model of Change developed by Prochaska and DiClemente (1984). This model delineates five stages of change that individuals must go through during the change process. These stages are:

1. Precontemplation
2. Contemplation
3. Preparation
4. Action
5. Maintenance

Precontemplation is characterized by the individual not seeing a problem. In people with substance use disorders, this is often common and may be mistakenly identified as denial (e.g., "I don't have a drinking problem.") Individuals in this stage may be unwilling or feel discouraged when it comes to change. They are not considering change in the near future (Velasquez, Maurer, Crouch, and DiClemente, 2001).

Contemplation is characterized by the individual seeing a problem but not considering action. They acknowledge that they have a problem and begin to think seriously about solving it. They have not yet made a commitment to change, however. Individuals may spend many years at this stage before they move to action or may never move to action at all. An example of this might be an individual who knows that smoking is a health risk and realizes that he or she should stop smoking, but they keep on doing it anyway.

Preparation has to do with making plans to change. People at this stage may be ready to change in the near future. Velasquez et al. (2001) state that those people at this stage change may have tried and failed to change before. They need to develop a plan that will work for them and make firm commitments to follow through on the action that they choose.

Action refers to the initiation of change behavior (such as entering a treatment program) and implementation of a plan. According to Velasquez et al. (2001), changes made during this stage are more visible to others and receive the greatest outward recognition. The authors caution that many people equate action with change, which may not always be accurate. Individuals in this stage still need a lot of support and encouragement.

Maintenance, the last stage, is one that focuses on sustaining the changes made in the previous stages. The primary goals of this stage are sustaining change and preventing relapse. Velasquez et al. (2001) also caution that without a strong commitment to maintenance activities, the person will most likely relapse. They suggest that a person may remain at this stage for six months to a lifetime. They also state that, even with an active process, a person may experience relapse and recycle through these stages many times before being successful at permanent change.

Most authors on co-occurring disorders recommend that specific treatment interventions be tailored to the stage of change that the client is currently in. For example, a client in the precontemplation change would benefit from motivational interviewing, while a client in the action stage would benefit more from cognitive-behavioral or skills training interventions (Mueser et al., 2003).

Prochaska and DiClemente (1984) identified ten specific processes of change that enable people to move from one stage to the next. Velasquez et al. (2001) report that these processes fall into two groups, experiential and behavioral:

I. Experiential Processes
    A. Consciousness raising (e.g., gaining knowledge of self and behaviors)
    B. Dramatic relief (e.g., emotional arousal)
    C. Self-reevaluation (e.g., how current behavior conflicts with personal goals)

    D. Reappraisal of behavior
    E. Environmental reevaluation (e.g., recognizing effects behavior has on others and the environment)
    F. Social liberation (e.g., recognition and creation of alternatives in social environment that encourage behavioral change)
II. Behavioral Processes
    A. Stimulus control (e.g., avoidance or alteration of cues so that it is less likely that the person will engage in problem behavior)
    B. Counterconditioning (e.g., substitution of healthy for unhealthy behaviors)
    C. Reinforcement management (e.g., rewarding of positive behavior changes)
    D. Self-liberation (e.g., belief in one's ability to change and acting on that belief by making a commitment to alter behavior)
    E. Helping relationships (e.g., relationships that provide support, caring, and acceptance to someone who is attempting to make a change)

The authors state that the above processes should be used at the right time in order to facilitate change from one stage to the next and offer several techniques for enhancing the change processes (Velasquez et al., 2001):

- Psychoeducation for consciousness raising, stimulus control, and social liberation
- Values clarification for self-reevaluation
- Problem solving for enhanced self-efficacy
- Goal-setting for self-liberation
- Relapse prevention planning to help with self-liberation by development of an action plan for change
- Relaxation techniques counterconditioning anxiety with calmness and awareness
- Assertion training enhances counterconditioning by providing healthy responses for clients to substitute in place of substance use in tempting situations
- Role play to enhance counterconditioning by providing healthy alternative behaviors in place of substance use
- Cognitive techniques to enhance consciousness raising, self-reevaluation, environmental reevaluation, self-liberation, counterconditioning, and reinforcement management
- Environmental restructuring including avoidance of high risk people, places, or situations that might cause temptation to use substances enhancing stimulus control

- Role clarification identifies how substance use has affected the various roles a person plays and enhances environmental reevaluation
- Reinforcement through reward enhances reinforcement management
- Social skills and communication skills enhancement helps to develop skills that will expand the client's support system
- Needs clarification enhances social liberation by identifying resources that can be utilized to maintain changes and improvements
- Assessment and feedback helps to raise consciousness by giving realistic feedback and data helpful in learning the impact or extent of substance use

The authors offer several exercises that can be used at the various stages of change that incorporate these techniques. The reader is encouraged to read this reference for specific exercises and techniques that can be used with their clients. Some modifications might be necessary to integrate these processes with clients who have co-occurring disorders.

COGNITIVE-BEHAVIORAL THERAPY

Cognitive-behavioral therapy (CBT) has been proven to be one of the most effective forms of treatment for most mental disorders (Beck and Rector, 2000; Beck, Rush, Shaw, and Emery, 1979). In addition, it has also been proven effective as a form of treatment for substance abuse (Beck et al., 1993). More recently, there has been a large body of research on the effectiveness of CBT with co-occurring disorders. Numerous authors have indicated that CBT is considered an essential element in the integrated treatment of co-occurring disorders because of the preponderance of evidence regarding the effectiveness of this form of therapy (Drake et al., 2004; Goldsmith and Garlapati, 2004; Mueser, Torrey, Lynde, Singer, and Drake, 2003; Brooks and Penn, 2003; Granholm et al., 2003; Barrowclough et al., 2001; Rach-Beisel et al., 1999; Bellack and Gearon, 1998).

Cognitive-behavioral therapy is based in the concept that a person responds to external and internal events depending upon their beliefs and thoughts about that event. This, in turn, results in an emotional response and physical behaviors to deal with those emotions. For example, people may receive criticism from their boss for their performance on a project. If these people believe that they are failures, their emotional reaction to the criticism will be filtered by that belief and the meaning they attach to that belief. The emotional response may be anger, depression, shame, guilt, or a host of other responses.

Consequently, their behavioral response may be to isolate and withdraw from others or to abuse drugs or alcohol to deal with their distress and negative emotions. The goal of CBT would be to identify the irrational belief and to refute it. The irrational belief would be substituted with a more rational or accurate belief, which should have an impact on the emotional response. This process is called cognitive restructuring. Additional CBT interventions can target the behavioral responses. For example, the client can learn positive coping skills to deal with stressful feelings and learn alternative behaviors. Instead of using substances to deal with stressful feelings, the client can be taught to go for a walk or call a friend to talk.

Beck et al. (1993) outline a cognitive theory of addictions. In that theory, they identify three different layers of beliefs: core beliefs, addictive beliefs, and permissive beliefs. In the example above the person's core belief is, "I am a failure." Their addictive belief may be "I need drugs/alcohol to feel better." A permissive belief is one that allows the person permission to use the substance or engage in the behavior. In the above example, the permissive belief may be "Go ahead and use, you will feel better." Beck and his colleagues theorize that this process may become automatic and happen so quickly, the client may not be able to intervene to stop the process. CBT can focus on helping the client to identify these different layers of beliefs and to develop strategies and behaviors to disrupt the cycle. One of the concerns expressed by Beck et al. (1993) is that traditional substance abuse treatment focuses on the addictive behavior and how to stop that behavior. What it may fail to do is to help the client to identify the core beliefs or to develop strategies for refuting those beliefs. Even if the person has successfully maintained abstinence from drugs/alcohol, they may still be prone to react with powerful urges and cravings to high-risk situations (people, places, and things). This is because their basic beliefs about the relative advantages and disadvantages of substance use have not changed substantially. While they may have developed adequate strategies for controlling their substance use, they may not have modified the attitudes and beliefs that fuel the craving, which can be triggered by high-risk situations. In short, their addictive beliefs have not changed and lie dormant until they are aroused in a high-risk situation. Permissive beliefs then resurface to allow the person to engage in the behavior (use).

Applying CBT to the treatment of substance abuse and co-occurring disorders usually involves multiple techniques such as social skills training, relapse prevention and refusal skills training, coping skills training, and psychoeducation. Goldsmith and Garlapati (2004) report that cognitive-behavioral treatment helps clients to develop new strategies and skills that will replace maladaptive patterns with healthy behaviors. They report that the key active ingredients of CBT are thought to be:

• Functional analysis of substance abuse
• Individualized training in recognizing and coping with craving, managing thoughts about substance use, problem solving, planning for emergencies, recognizing seemingly irrelevant decisions, and refusal skills
• Examination of the patient's cognitive processes related to substance use
• Identification and debriefing of past and future high-risk situations
• Encouragement and review of extra session implementation of skills
• Practice of skills within sessions

Brooks and Penn (2003) describe a specific form of CBT developed for use with dual diagnosis patients called Self-Management and Recovery Training (SMART). SMART is a structured format that involves material on mental illness management, relapse prevention, goal setting, survival skills, written assignments, weekend preparation, and recreation. The SMART program was effective in reducing substance use and reducing psychiatric symptoms and psychiatric hospitalizations. Drake et al. (2004) reviewed several studies that showed positive outcomes such as decreased substance abuse and psychiatric symptoms when CBT was used.

Bellack and Gearon (1998) and Bellack and DiClemente (1999) describe a specifically targeted treatment program for substance abusing schizophrenics called Behavioral Treatment for Substance Abuse in Schizophrenia (BTSAS) consisting of four modules that are implemented sequentially:

• Social skills and problem-solving training to enable patients to develop nonsubstance-using social contacts and be able to refuse social pressure to use substances
• Education about the reasons for substance use (e.g., habits, triggers, and craving) and the particular dangers of substance use for people with schizophrenia in order to shift decisional balance toward decreased use; motivational interviewing and goal setting to identify realistic short-term goals for decreased substance use
• Training in behavioral skills for coping with urges and high risk situations and relapse prevention skills

The modules are presented in a small group, and material is presented in didactic and behavioral rehearsal formats.

Weiss, Griffin, Greenfield, Najavits, Wyner, and Soto (2000) developed a manual-based program for bipolar patients with a substance use disorder. They called it IGT or Integrated Group Therapy. It consisted of twenty weekly sessions that included topics on substance abuse and bipolar disorder, identifying substance use triggers, depression and mania, coping mechanisms for dealing with triggers, managing mood changes without substances, improving relationships with family and friends, understanding denial and ambivalence about both disorders, recognizing warning signs of relapse into substance use or mood symptoms, how to refuse alcohol/drugs, using self-help groups, taking medications for bipolar and substance use disorders, thinking in ways that are characteristic of recovery rather than relapse, self-care, balancing recovery with other demands, developing healthy relationships, weighing the pros and cons of recovery, continuing recovery after completing the group, and stabilizing recovery.

Mueser et al. (2003) describe four stages of treatment: (1) engagement; (2) persuasion; (3) active treatment; and (4) relapse prevention. They suggest pairing certain cognitive-behavioral interventions with the specific stage the client is in. These stages of treatment are closely tied to the stages of change (Prochaska and DiClemente, 1994) mentioned previously.

Mueser et al. (2003) suggest that in the engagement stage, the cognitive-behavioral interventions should focus on altering verbal behavior, not the substance use behavior, by focusing on reinforcing clear communication about substance use without altering the use itself. The persuasion stage utilizes motivational interviewing to help the client develop an understanding of the pattern of events surrounding substance use and its consequences in order to increase motivation to change substance use behaviors. In the active treatment stage, the goal is to teach the client the skills necessary for reducing substance use and achieving abstinence, combined with better illness management. The relapse prevention stage focuses on refining the behavioral action plan and on altering elements of the client's lifestyle that could lead to relapse. The behavioral action plan includes specific action goals such as sobriety, medication compliance, managing cravings, and managing relapse.

Monti, Kadden, Rossenow, Cooney, and Abrams (2002) have developed a coping skills guide for treating alcohol dependence. There are specific suggestions for working with persons who have co-occurring disorders. They delineate the following cognitive-behavioral interventions for treating specific disorders (163–73).

Depression:

• Increasing awareness of negative thoughts, depressive symptoms, and their relation to alcohol use; refuting cognitive distortions (e.g., managing negative thinking; anger management; receiving criticism)

- Developing skills to cope with various negative situations (e.g., problem solving)
- Organizing a schedule of pleasant activities
- Improving interpersonal skills and enhancing social support (e.g., assertiveness, conversation skills, giving and receiving positive feedback, developing social support networks)

Anxiety Disorders:

- Emphasizing general cognitive therapy sessions (e.g., managing negative thinking, anger management, problem solving)
- Emphasizing social skills useful for social phobia (e.g., conversational skills, nonverbal behavior, assertiveness, developing social support networks, drink refusal skills)
- Cueing exposure with urge-specific coping skills training
- Utilizing anxiety-provoking cues in exposure therapy (e.g., systematic desensitization)
- Avoiding use of medications with abuse potential

Psychotic Disorders:

- Emphasizing basic social skills building sessions (e.g., conversational skills, nonverbal behavior, developing social support networks, drink refusal skills, giving and receiving positive feedback)
- Enhancing social supports and structuring of time (e.g., developing social support networks, increasing pleasant activities)
- Utilizing harm reduction and motivational interviewing approaches for clients who are not in an action stage of change

Personality Disorders:

- Modulating negative emotions (e.g., managing negative thinking, anger management)
- Increasing positive events (e.g., increasing pleasant activities)
- Enhancing interpersonal effectiveness (e.g., assertiveness, giving constructive criticism, receiving criticism, giving and receiving positive feedback, anger management)
- Solving problems and making decisions (e.g., problem solving, seemingly irrelevant decisions)
- Coping skills training to prevent relapses (e.g., drink refusal skills, managing urges to drink, and cue exposure with the urge-specific coping skills training)

Linehan et al. (1999) described a cognitive-behavioral program for treating a borderline personality disorder, Dialectical Behavioral Therapy, which includes behavioral skills training in the following areas: developing distress tolerance, identifying and modulating negative emotions, increasing positive events, enhancing personal effectiveness, problem solving, self-management, decision-making, communication skills, relapse prevention, and cognitive restructuring. In addition, for clients with co-occurring substance use disorders, there are modules on relapse prevention, replacement medication pharmacotherapy, and interventions to enhance the alliance between the client and the therapist.

Bellack et al. (1997) produced a step-by-step guide for social skills training for persons with schizophrenia. The guide outlines forty-eight specific social skills that can help improve the patients functioning. While the reader is encouraged to read this guide to get a more comprehensive overview of the specific skills and the curricula for teaching these skills to clients, the following is a partial list of the primary skill areas:

- Conversation skills
- Conflict management skills
- Assertiveness skills
- Community living skills
- Friendship and dating skills
- Medication management skills
- Vocational/work skills

The authors identify several social skills in the curriculum that can be used with clients who have a co-occurring substance use disorder. They are:

- Making requests
- Refusing requests
- How to disagree without arguing
- Getting your point across
- Compromising and negotiation
- Listening to others
- Solving problems

As has been previously stated, these interventions work best when combined with other integrated treatment approaches, such as motivational interviewing, medication management, case management, and family interventions. They should be tailored to the individual client and the specific stage of change and/or stage of treatment that the client is in at any particular time. This requires ongoing client assessment and flexibility in the treatment process. While abstinence from substance use is the recommended goal, clients with co-occurring disorders may not accept or be ready to discontinue their substance use. Therefore, harm reduction strategies and flexible approaches to treatment, such as persuasion groups or motivational counseling, should be available and practiced (Carey et al., 2002).

12-STEP APPROACHES

The foundation of most substance abuse treatment programs and recovery support is the 12-step model originally developed in Alcoholics Anonymous (AA, 1953). While developed as a self-help program, many treatment programs have adopted this same model for treating substance abusers. These programs help clients to work the steps and begin this process during their treatment with the goal of linking them to community-based support groups for ongoing recovery support. Many other self-help programs have modeled themselves after the AA model. Much research has been done on the effectiveness of this approach in treating substance abuse and some research has been done on the effectiveness of this approach with individuals who have a co-occurring disorder. Brooks and Penn (2003) compared the effectiveness of 12-step vs. SMART training (a cognitive-behavioral approach). They found that the 12-step intervention was more effective at decreasing alcohol use and increasing social interactions, but the clients in the 12-step intervention showed a worsening of medical problems, health status, employment status, and psychiatric hospitalizations. The authors cite other studies that showed positive outcomes with the 12-step approach, the most significant being a reduction in substance use for persons actively participating in 12-step groups for at least one year. Drake et al. (2004) reviewed several studies on treatment outcomes for people with co-occurring disorders. They found that 12-step approaches were about as effective as other approaches for reducing substance use in this population but not as effective in reducing other problems that were related to psychiatric disorders. In short, it appears that treatment programs incorporating a mixture of treatment strategies including 12-step, cognitive-behavioral, and motivational interventions, have the best outcomes with dually diagnosed clients.

Initially, the 12-step program was developed as a self-help program rather than a form of treatment. It was because of the success of this program in helping alcoholics (and eventually other substance abusers) succeed in achieving and maintaining sobriety that many treatment programs adapted this approach to their clinical programs. Generally, most people with substance use disorders are encouraged to participate in community-based self-help programs. Minkoff (2000) encourages participation in some form of 12-

step support program to help stabilize substance use problems that can exacerbate mental illness. Other authors have expressed concerns about clients with dual disorders participating in traditional 12-step self-help groups (Mueser et al., 2003; Bellack and Gearon, 1998).

Mueser and his colleagues identified both advantages and disadvantages of traditional 12-step based groups:

Advantages:

- No cost
- Diverse membership
- Accessibility
- Acceptance
- Value system
- Consistency
- Support

Disadvantages:

- Focus on abstinence from the start
- Strong spiritual orientation
- Potential difficulty relating to losses experienced by other group members
- Some members hostile to psychiatric medications
- Problems assimilating due to social skill deficits

Others have expressed similar concerns due to the confrontational approach taken by many of these groups (Carey et al., 2000) and the specific aspects of certain mental illnesses (cognitive deficits, hallucinations and/or delusions, social skill deficits, agoraphobia, social phobia) that make participation in these programs difficult or impossible.

Noordsy, Schwab, and Fox (1996) found that clients with co-occurring affective disorders are more likely to benefit from participation in self-help groups than persons with schizophrenia. This is likely due to the negative symptoms and cognitive deficits found in persons with schizophrenia. Mueser et al. (2003) recommend that all appropriate clients should explore self-help groups as an adjunct to treatment.

There have been some specialized 12-step programs developed for people with co-occurring disorders. Programs like Dual Recovery Anonymous or Double Trouble in Recovery are designed to help participants recover from both disorders and emphasize both in their meetings. They are more accepting of mental illness, the use of medications, and the interplay between both disorders. One study by Laudet, Magura, Cleland, Vogel, Knight, and Rosenblum (2004) looked at participants in a Double Trouble in Recovery program over the course of a two-year period and found that ongoing attendance in this program significantly increased the likelihood that a participant would be abstinent from alcohol or drugs. This specialized form of integrated self-help has proven itself successful in clients with dual disorders.

An example of such an integrated approach can be found in *The Twelve Steps and Dual Disorders* (Hamilton and Samples, 1995). In this workbook the authors outline and rework the original 12-steps (AA, 1953) in an integrated way to identify and acknowledge both disorders. The following is taken from that workbook:

1. Admitted we were powerless over our dual illness of chemical dependency and emotional of psychiatric illness—that our lives had become unmanageable.
2. Came to believe that a Higher Power of our understanding could restore us to sanity.
3. Made a decision to turn our will and our lives over to the care of our Higher Power, to help us to rebuild our lives in a positive and caring way.
4. Made a searching and fearless personal inventory of ourselves.
5. Admitted to our Higher Power, to ourselves, and to another human being, the exact nature of our liabilities and our assets.
6. Were entirely ready to have our Higher Power remove all our liabilities.
7. Humbly asked our Higher Power to remove these liabilities and to help us to strengthen our assets for recovery.
8. Made a list of all persons we had harmed and became willing to make amends to them all.
9. Made direct amends to such people wherever possible, except when to do so would injure them or others.
10. Continued to take personal inventory and when wrong, promptly admitted it while continuing to recognize our progress in dual recovery.
11. Sought through prayer and meditation to improve our conscious contact with our Higher Power, praying only for knowledge of our Higher Power's will for us and the power to carry that out.
12. Having had a spiritual awakening as a result of these Steps, we tried to carry this message to others who experience dual disorders and to practice these principles in all our affairs. (43)

There are also self-help groups other than the traditional 12-step-based groups that are available to clients. While not specific to co-occurring disorders, they may be attractive to certain clients due to their lack of emphasis on spirituality and surrendering to a higher power, which may turn some clients away.

One such group is Rational Recovery (Trimpey, 1996). It does not require abstinence in order to participate and places emphasis on self-responsibility rather
on spirituality. For many with co-occurring disorders this may be a viable option. Mueser et al. (2003) point out that the availability of these groups is less
than traditional AA groups; therefore, access may be a problem.

Chapter Seven

Clinical Vignettes

This chapter includes several brief clinical vignettes. These are actual and/or representative cases of clients with co-occurring disorders. Each case highlights the complexities of assessment and treatment. The suggested assessment and treatment strategies are not meant to be comprehensive; rather, they are designed to present a basic overview of an integrated treatment process. Readers may want to use these vignettes for discussion or training purposes and are encouraged to pull treatment strategies and interventions from the many listed in this book.

Randall

Randall is a thirty-two-year-old Caucasian single male. He was referred by the court to substance abuse treatment following an arrest for possession of methamphetamine. He also has a previous arrest for driving under the influence of alcohol (DUI). Upon admission to the substance abuse treatment program, Randall presents with loud and pressured speech, increased irritability and difficulty sitting still. He seems agitated. His last use of methamphetamine was reportedly one week ago and his last use of alcohol was reportedly more than seventy-two hours ago. During the assessment interview, Randall seems hypertalkative, and his thoughts seem to be coming so fast that it is hard to follow him. He seems preoccupied with the police and feels like they "have it out for him." He blames them for all of his current troubles and suspects that they have been following him for some time. He is convinced that the police "planted" the drugs in his car. He has never had any previous treatment or therapy and does not feel like he "deserves to be treated this way." He does not believe that he has a drug or alcohol problem. He reports that he only uses drugs "occasionally," and he drinks alcohol mostly on weekends "like everyone else."

Assessment and Treatment Issues

Randall's current mental status is of concern. His pressured speech, agitation, and paranoia could be symptomatic of his methamphetamine use, although he claims that he has not used methamphetamine in over seventy-two hours. A urine or blood drug screen would determine if Randall still had the drug (or other substances) in his system. At this point in the process he might not be willing to cooperate with a drug screen. Confronting him while he is in such an agitated and paranoid state could cause him to become aggressive and hostile. A calm and assertive approach would probably be the best one. Even if he has not used methamphetamines in the last few days, it is not uncommon for residual psychological symptoms to be present. Paranoia and other thought disturbances can continue for several weeks or months following the cessation of drug use. Randall's alcohol use should also be assessed as some of his symptoms and behavior could be related to alcohol intoxication or withdrawal. If it is determined that Randall's altered mental status is not the result of substance use, then it is likely that he has a mental illness. Since he has not had a previous history of treatment for or diagnosis of a mental illness, a psychiatric evaluation should be conducted as soon as possible. Randall's symptom presentation correlates with several mental disorders including bipolar disorder and schizophrenia. While a specific diagnosis may take some time to determine, it is clear that he will need some type of psychiatric intervention. Given his current level of resistance and denial about his substance use and poor reality testing, it may be difficult to engage Randall in any treatment. There may be some leverage that can be used from the court, since they were the ones who ordered Randall to receive treatment. While coercing treatment does not necessarily produce poor outcomes, it might be more prudent to attempt to engage him with motivational interviewing techniques. This might involve one-on-one sessions with a clinician aimed at exploring Randall's resistance and ambivalence. Randall is clearly a "precontemplator" and thus not ready for any significant treatment interventions. Actually, forcing too much on him at this time might increase his resistance and feed his paranoia. The goal would be to get Randall to agree to further assessment and evaluation while looking at the "possibility" that there may be more significant problems that need to be addressed (e.g., his substance use and mental health issues). In an integrated approach we can address his substance use and psychiatric issues at the same time. Once he is engaged we can begin to intervene on both levels. Since Randall is still in denial of his alcohol and drug use problems, he might be more willing to accept that there are psychiatric problems that need to be addressed. Getting him started on appropriate medications and continuing motivational interviewing sessions will move him to a higher "readiness" to change. As his psychiatric symptoms stabilize and decrease, he can be transitioned to groups designed for clients in the earlier stages of change. The goal would be to help Randall begin to look at his alcohol and drug use and the impact that it is having on his life. If Randall was "forced" to undergo traditional substance abuse treatment, he would likely fail given his agitation, paranoia, and general resistance and denial. While many people enter substance abuse treatment through coercion, that alone does not preclude a positive treatment outcome.

While it could be argued that Randall is similar to most methamphetamine and alcohol abusers, his chances of treatment success will be enhanced by conducting a more comprehensive assessment and by engaging him in the treatment process. The use of appropriate psychotropic medication to decrease his agitation and paranoia should be a major focus of early treatment regardless of whether it is the result of substance use or a mental illness. Motivational strategies can be utilized to address his substance use and move him toward active treatment. Once he is engaged in the treatment process, specific interventions can be utilized to assist him in addressing his substance use and psychiatric problems. Time will tell if Randall's paranoia and other symptoms are more related to his drug use or if he has a co-occurring mental illness. If his symptoms clear rapidly then it is more likely that they are related to his drug use. He would still benefit from integrated treatment interventions. Cognitive-behavioral strategies, such as cost-benefit analysis and other psychoeducational approaches, can help him to realistically evaluate the effects of his drug and alcohol use. Helping him to look at the financial, social, legal, and psychological consequences of his substance use may help to enhance his motivation to not use. Of course any reality impairment caused from a mental disorder could inhibit any progress in this area and must be addressed first.

Melinda

Melinda is a twenty-eight-year-old African-American female who is single. She has one child, a seven-year-old, who lives with Melinda's mother. Melinda has struggled on and off with crack cocaine use. She began using crack in her late teens. She dropped out of high school. For a while she worked as a housekeeper in the same hotel as her mother. She stopped working after she got pregnant and had her child. At that time she applied and received public assistance. During her pregnancy she did not use drugs or drink alcohol. After having her child, Melinda became seriously depressed and withdrawn. She began to drink heavily. Her mother saw that Melinda was not able to take care of her child. She relinquished the care of her child to her mother until she "could get it together." Melinda continued to drink heavily and eventually resumed the use of crack cocaine. As time went on, Melinda started to have problems organizing her thoughts. At times she would almost sound incoherent. This was especially true after using alcohol and drugs, but the disorganized thinking persisted long after the effects of the drugs wore off. Melinda withdrew into herself. She began to hear voices, and she would engage in elaborate conversations with these voices. It was as if she perceived the voices to be those of real people. Melinda found that drinking alcohol and using crack cocaine initially would help to diminish her anxiety and quiet the voices; however, they would return with a vengeance when the drugs wore off. The situation continued to worsen when her mother found her in her apartment curled up in a fetal position talking to herself. She had not eaten or bathed for several days. Melinda was hospitalized at a local hospital in the psychiatric unit.

Assessment and Treatment Issues

Initially the focus of treatment will be on stabilizing Melinda's psychiatric condition. This will likely be done by administering appropriate antipsychotic medications. During this time the clinical team can also evaluate and manage any withdrawal symptoms from the alcohol and crack cocaine use. A complete medical evaluation should be conducted since Melinda has not been eating or caring for herself for some time. It appears as if she has been using the drugs to self-medicate her psychiatric symptoms. Ironically, the drugs have likely worsened her condition rather than made it better. As her condition stabilizes, she can begin to receive individual, group, and family interventions. It will be important to assess Melinda's motivation level regarding her substance use and her mental illness. Since she has no previous treatment history, she may respond well to education regarding both her substance use and mental illness. The initial focus will be on engaging her in the need for ongoing treatment. The clinician can help her to look at the "costs" of her substance use (her relationship with her daughter and inability to work) and the relationship between her substance use and her mental illness (it makes the voices and depression worse). It may be useful to involve Melinda's mother in family counseling to assist in improving the relationship with her mother and daughter. By restoring her to a more functional level, Melinda may be able to play a more significant role in parenting her daughter. Teaching Melinda about the need for medication and medication compliance coupled with the need to avoid alcohol and drugs will be extremely important. Melinda may need some form of specialized residential treatment for her substance use. Her ability to tolerate a more traditional substance treatment program will need to be assessed, as her mental illness symptoms might cause her to be uncomfortable and not appropriate for that type of setting. A more integrated type of program or one that is sensitive to persons with co-occurring disorders may be a better choice, if available. A structured residential program can also help Melinda develop independent living skills while supporting her sobriety. It is highly likely that she will experience strong cravings to use crack cocaine or drink alcohol. She will need to learn how to manage these cravings. She will also need to develop skills at managing stress and depression, conflict and problem resolution, relapse prevention, and others to name a few. Referral to an ongoing support group would also be indicated. A group that recognizes both substance use and mental illness would be the best; however, if unavailable, Melinda would need to experiment with her comfort level in either a traditional 12-step group such as Narcotics Anonymous or Cocaine Anonymous. Another option might be a group such as National Alliance for the Mentally Ill (NAMI) that would be more focused on her mental illness but is often sensitive to all of the manifestations of mental disorders including substance abuse.

Carlos

Carlos is a thirty-four-year-old Hispanic male. He was married for five years but is now divorced. He has two small children who live with his ex-wife. He visits them as "often as he can" but is inconsistent. Carlos began drinking alcohol and smoking "weed" in his early teens. Initially he started using it as a way to fit in socially, but he quickly found that it helped him to forget about his problems at home. His father was an alcoholic and was abusive to Carlos's mother and siblings. Carlos's mother was depressed most of the time and did not provide much emotional nurturing or support to Carlos or his siblings. Carlos also suffered from bouts of depression but never sought help or discussed his problems with anyone. He kept his personal and family problems to himself. As Carlos grew older, he continued to regularly drink alcohol and smoke marijuana. He prided himself on his ability to drink more than his friends. Despite his heavy drinking and smoking, Carlos held a job and eventually married his high school sweetheart. She was aware of Carlos's drinking but did not say much about it as it was something "all the guys" were doing. During a period of difficult economic times, Carlos was laid off from his job. He became very depressed and began drinking heavily on a daily basis. His wife would come home from her job and find him drunk or passed out on the sofa. They would argue intensely about his drinking. The longer he was laid off, the more depressed he became and the more he would drink. Eventually the tension became too much, and Carlos and his wife separated. His wife could no longer tolerate his drinking. She gave him an ultimatum to get help, or she would divorce him. Reluctantly Carlos started to attend Alcoholics Anonymous meetings, and over time he was able to stop drinking. His wife saw the change in him and moved back in the house. He was called back to his old job. For several months, things seemed to have gotten better. Carlos became busy with his responsibilities at home and at work. He started to attend AA less and less. It was about this time when he learned that his mother was very ill and might not live. He was devastated and became tearful and depressed. As his mother's condition worsened, so did his depression. To cope with his feelings Carlos began to drink again. At first he would stop off after work for "one or two beers," but it was not long until he was drinking as heavily as before. Carlos' wife could not handle the frustration and uncertainty. She moved out of the house and filed for divorce. This sent Carlos into a deeper depression. He got to the point where he considered committing suicide. He felt desperate and hopeless.

Assessment and Treatment Issues

The most important issue with Carlos is to determine his risk level for suicide. This would be done by conducting a risk assessment. If he is considered a high risk, then steps should be taken to maintain his safety. Typically this would involve psychiatric hospitalization. This would take priority over any other interventions.

Carlos is a fairly typical client in many respects. As we look at his history, it is unclear if the alcohol and drug use preceded the depression or if the depression exacerbated the drug and alcohol use. Given that there is a family history of both alcohol and depression, there is certainly a predisposition for both problems. It is clear that as his drug and alcohol use increased, his level of depression also increased. It is also true that when Carlos stopped drinking and attending AA, his depression seemed to lift. Interestingly, his depression seemed to return as he struggled to cope with his mother's illness. This led to a relapse of the alcohol use that in turn made his depression even worse. Clients like Carlos will present themselves in many different treatment scenarios. If they believe that their depression is the main problem, then they may present in a mental health setting. If they are focused on their alcohol and drug use, they may present in a substance abuse treatment setting. In either case, failure to assess the co-occurring problems will likely cause a relapse of both problems. Depression is common among alcoholics. Sometimes the depression is temporary and will lift within a few weeks. In Carlos's case there is a long history of depression and substance use. While the depression did lift when the substance use stopped, there seemed to be a return of the depression when sober. In an integrated approach, both problems would be assessed and treatment would be directed at managing both. It is important for Carlos to see the relationship between the depression and substance use as he will have to manage both disorders.

Treatment will likely involve antidepressants due to the severity and recurrent nature of the depression. The use of antidepressants to treat milder or more transient situational depression may not be necessary. Cognitive-behavioral psychotherapy has been shown to be an equally effective treatment for this type of depression and can be used in conjunction with medication for the more severe forms of depression. Getting Carlos back to AA is also important. He found success there in the past. He will likely need ongoing support to maintain his sobriety and to help him through his mother's illness. It will be important to reassess Carlos's suicide risk on an ongoing basis. Since his depression seems to be reactive to real and perceived losses in his environment, things will likely rise and fall based upon external events. A solid recovery program with AA can help him to manage these unplanned events.

Family therapy and/or couples therapy may help Carlos to deal with his mother's illness, his family history of abuse, and his relationship issues with his ex-wife. It is unclear about the status of Carlos's marriage. Unresolved relationship issues have been a relapse trigger in the past and will likely pose a problem in the future.

JoAnn

JoAnn is a twenty-nine-year-old Caucasian single female. She is addicted to vicodin. She began taking vicodin for pain following foot surgery. She liked how it made her feel. Not only did it reduce her physical pain but it also reduced her emotional pain. She had never told anyone about her childhood. From age ten to thirteen, she was sexually molested by her stepfather. She never told her mother because she was afraid that it would upset her too much and that the family would have to move away and be homeless. Her stepfather would tell her that her mother would never believe her if she told. JoAnn knew what was happening to her was wrong, but she kept silent. She used to pretend to be asleep when her stepfather would enter her room. As he would molest her, she would pretend that she was dreaming and would think about her favorite things. She learned to disassociate, which helped her to cope with what was happening to her. When she reached puberty, the molestation suddenly stopped. Even though the molestation had stopped, JoAnn was still filled with fear that her stepfather would return to molest her again. She was filled with shame and anger that she could not express. Her anger turned to rage. She began to act out. Her grades in school declined. She became rebellious and started experimenting with alcohol and drugs. For awhile she became sexually promiscuous. All the while she felt more alone and depressed. It was then that she started to cut herself on the tops of her forearms. During the cutting she would disassociate, like she had done before when her stepfather was molesting her. The cutting helped to release the anger and rage that had built up inside her. By the time she was sixteen, she knew she was in trouble. Her mother was still unaware of the molestation but knew that something was wrong with JoAnn. She took JoAnn to a psychiatrist who diagnosed her with depression and prescribed antidepressant medications. JoAnn did not tell the psychiatrist about the molestation or the cutting. The medication did help somewhat and the cutting lessened. She still felt empty and alone. Secretly she felt dirty and full of shame. Her early twenties were full of intense relationships that never seemed to last. She was still full of rage and would express it in angry outbursts followed by periods of deep depression and emptiness. She would often engage in periods of self-destructive behaviors, such as drinking excessively, driving recklessly, and engaging in "risky" sexual behavior. At twenty-six, JoAnn was drunk and having an argument with her boyfriend when she stumbled and fell off a curb. She fractured her ankle and broke a bone in her foot. She was in intense pain for several weeks, and the doctor prescribed vicodin for her pain. JoAnn found that the vicodin not only relieved her physical pain but also eased her emotional pain. She began to require larger amounts of the medication as her tolerance grew. She began to see several doctors to get her medication in order to not arouse suspicion. She would often mix the vicodin with alcohol that would cause her to become hostile and depressed. It was during one of these episodes that she got into an intense argument with a boyfriend. She became violent and threw him out of the house. After he left, she attempted suicide by taking an overdose of her medications. In a stupor she called her boyfriend to tell him what she had done. He contacted the authorities, and they took her to the emergency room for treatment. After learning that this was a suicide attempt, the emergency room doctor transferred JoAnn to the psychiatric unit under a seventy-two-hour emergency hold.

Assessment and Treatment Issues

JoAnn's case is an all too common one for young women (and men) who have experienced early childhood trauma, especially sexual abuse. Many women who develop substance use disorders and mental illness have experienced some type of early trauma. In JoAnn's situation, the repeated sexual molestation by her stepfather was made worse by her inability to express to her mother or anyone else what was happening to her. Without early intervention, JoAnn was left to carry the emotional pain of her abuse. Unable to express this pain she turned to self-destructive behaviors, such as alcohol and drug abuse, sexual acting out, and finally cutting. She also learned early on how to disassociate, which is a common "survival" mechanism for victims of trauma and abuse.

JoAnn's clinical picture is complex and mixed. She meets the criteria for borderline personality disorder. Given her traumatic history she may also be experiencing Post-Traumatic Stress Disorder. It is also likely that she does experience periods of major depression as well. All of these problems are exacerbated by her alcohol and drug use and especially by her vicodin dependency. JoAnn's prognosis for "recovery" from these conditions is guarded. Very often people with her clinical profile do not respond well to traditional psychotherapy, medications, or substance abuse treatment. Clearly, the best approach for JoAnn would be an integrated one. With an integrated approach, we could begin the withdrawal of the vicodin during her hospital stay. This would likely involve the administration of buprenorphine, which suppresses opiate withdrawal symptoms. During this time we can begin to involve her in psychoeducational groups for clients in the early stages of change (precontemplation, contemplation, and preparation). These groups would focus on both her substance use and her emotional/behavioral issues. The goal would be to motivate JoAnn to the "action" stage where she was ready and willing to make the necessary changes to her behavior. Since JoAnn has never dealt with her sexual abuse trauma, it would be helpful to begin exploring this in individual and group psychotherapy sessions. In some clients this will trigger strong emotional reactions that may or may not be therapeutic. Many clients with borderline personality disorder are unable to regulate their emotions, and thus bringing up intense emotional content may trigger a crisis. On the other hand, not exploring the client's deeper emotional content may prevent her from resolving her problems and moving forward. The treatment team will have to continually evaluate JoAnn's response to various emotional content and expression. It may be that JoAnn would be appropriate for a form of cognitive-behavioral therapy called dialectical behavioral therapy. It is designed to effectively treat clients with borderline personality disorder. It would focus on behavioral skills training, emotional regulation, problem solving, and relapse prevention. Therapy will have to be ongoing and will at times be crisis-oriented. JoAnn might benefit from involvement in some form of 12-step support group. The structure and support of this type of program may be helpful, although they can also be a source of conflict and "drama" for someone with BPD. An integrated multidisciplinary team approach toward treating this

client will produce the best results, with continual monitoring and reassess-
ment of her response and compliance with various interventions.

Alan

Alan is a fifty-four-year-old African-American male who is divorced. He
lives alone in an apartment. He is an autoworker who works at a local factory
assembly plant. He was found hiding under his bed in his apartment, considered psychotic and experiencing visual hallucinations and paranoid delusions.
He believed that there were people outside of his apartment that were following him and trying to kill him. He saw them hiding in the bushes and be-
hind cars that were parked in the lot outside. At times Alan's speech was almost incoherent. He had been hiding under his bed for almost three days and
was found by a friend who came to check on him because Alan had missed
work during this time. He has no prior history of psychiatric or substance
abuse treatment. He was brought in to the emergency room of a local hospital by the police on an emergency seventy-two-hour psychiatric hold.

Assessment and Treatment Issues

Based upon Alan's presentation with severe psychotic symptoms, including
visual hallucinations and paranoid delusions and his bizarre behavior, it
would be easy and probably likely that he would be assessed with a severe
psychiatric disorder such as schizophrenia. This would be the case because
without the awareness that comes from cross-training in dual disorders, it
would not occur to most clinicians to look beyond the presenting symptoms.
In fact as Alan was brought in to the ER manifesting the above symptoms, he
was bypassed by the medical staff and sent directly to the mental health clinician for a mental health evaluation. Normally the ER medical staff evalu-
ates and clears the patient before calling in the mental health consult, but in
Alan's case they were sure that he was a "psych patient." As the mental health
clinician began to gather relevant information and history, he was puzzled
that Alan had never had any previous history of mental illness or psychiatric
treatment. The fact that he had a very good job and had many years of stable
employment also did not fit with someone with a long history of mental illness. Given Alan's age, fifty-four, the mental health clinician was concerned
that the acute onset of such severe psychiatric symptoms at this age could be
the sign of some type of medical or organic condition. The clinician, who was
cross-trained in assessing and treating substance use disorders, was also concerned about some type of substance use causing these symptoms and behaviors. Whether it was from training and experience or from some deeper intu-

ition, the clinician began to focus on the onset of the symptoms and behavior approximately three days prior to arriving at the hospital. For some reason the clinician put together the acute onset of symptoms, the client's age, and his occupation (the factory workers in the area were known to have a high incidence of substance use disorders) with severe alcohol withdrawal, known as delirium tremens or DTs. This condition is potentially life-threatening if not treated and usually develops within two to three days following the cessation of the use of alcohol. The clinician asked the emergency room staff to medically assess the client and expressed his concerns about possible DTs. To the ER staff's surprise, Alan's vital signs were indicative of someone in acute alcohol withdrawal. His blood pressure was seriously elevated, he had a temperature, he was dehydrated, and his mental status was seriously altered. The ER staff began to treat Alan immediately, and soon his symptoms began to decrease and his vital signs began to normalize. He was stabilized in the ER and transferred to a medical unit for observation. Within a couple of days, Alan's mental status had returned to normal. He was no longer psychotic. He admitted to a serious drinking problem and was referred to a substance abuse treatment program, which he was willing to do after he heard the story of how he came to be in the hospital in the first place.

This story highlights the importance of accurate assessment of the client. It is easy to assume that a client's symptoms define the problem. This is not the case, especially when there are co-occurring conditions. In Alan's case, he presented with what appeared to be a serious psychiatric disorder. Had he been admitted to the psychiatric unit treatment for his potentially life-threatening condition, treatment of his DT may have been delayed. The clinician should remember that every psychiatric symptom can be caused by a medical condition or by substance intoxication/withdrawal. The clinician should be especially concerned if the client is older (ages forty-five to fifty and older) and/or has an acute onset of psychiatric symptoms with no previous history. Whenever possible, clinicians should routinely utilize low cost and reliable drug and alcohol testing kits to screen for the presence of substances that can effect the client's behavior and mental status. This is one of the easiest ways to identify co-occurring disorders and to verify their level of adherence to sobriety.

Tina

Tina is a forty-four-year-old Hispanic female, married with two adult children who are twenty-two and twenty-six. Tina has a long history of depression and has had periods of psychosis throughout her adult life. She has had multiple psychiatric hospitalizations and has been on medications or in psychiatric treatment on and off for many years. In spite of her mental illness, Tina has managed to stay married to her husband and raise her two children. What Tina has never told anyone, including her doctor, is that she has been using some form of "speed" since she was nine years old. She primarily snorts or smokes it. She has taken pills as well. She and her husband have been using together for many years. He has been arrested and was put on probation for possession of drug paraphernalia. Tina and her husband stopped using for a while, but they resumed their use after the husband got off of probation. Tina reports that using the speed while taking her meds causes her to become paranoid. She also reports that using helps her get through the day and gives her energy. Otherwise she becomes depressed. She is ambivalent about quitting "speed." She does not think that she can. She also has not experienced significant negative consequences for her use that she can identify. It is unclear how much of her mental illness is related to her drug use and how much her drug use causes or exacerbates her mental illness. She verbalizes a desire to stop using "because of the example it sets for my grandchildren."

Assessment and Treatment Issues

Tina's case is very typical of many who have received or are receiving traditional mental health treatment. While she has been diagnosed and treated for her mental illness, she has never been assessed or treated for her use of speed. It is unclear how much her psychiatric symptoms have been exacerbated by drug use or how much her drug use has interfered with her psychiatric treatment and medications. In Tina's case, her use of "speed" began at an early age, long before the onset of her psychiatric problems. Given the age of early onset of her drug use, it would be important to further assess Tina for any history of physical or sexual abuse. Undiagnosed trauma can lead to relapse of both substance use and mental illness. Given her long history of depression and periods of psychosis, it is difficult to determine the nature and extent of her mental illness until she stops using "speed." Capitalizing on her motivation to stop using "because of the example it sets" for her grandchildren, we could begin an integrated assessment and treatment approach. It will be very difficult to get her to stop using drugs while her husband is actively using it. If he is unwilling or unable to stop using, then it may be necessary for Tina to enter a sober living environment or consider some form of residential treatment. The latter approach might be more beneficial as it would allow for a more controlled setting in which a thorough assessment can be completed. It would be important to get a baseline determination of her psychiatric symptoms and either adjust or reevaluate her current medication regimen. In a residential setting, Tina could be more closely monitored as she experiences any withdrawal symptoms from the speed. We would likely see an increase in fatigue and depression, which are common during the withdrawal from stimulants. There may also be an increase in paranoia and other psychotic symptoms. If the symptoms are more related to the drug use, they should begin to decrease within a few days to a few weeks. If they are related to or exacerbated by an underlying mental illness, then they should remain the same or increase.

As she is being stabilized, it will be important to keep her motivation level high so that she will engage in the treatment process. Separation from her husband and family will likely put pressure on her to return home. If possible, the family should also be engaged in the treatment process. As treatment progresses, Tina will have to learn how to cope with intense drug cravings, increased fatigue, and depression. She will need to be taught how to manage both her substance use disorder and her mental illness.

Given Tina's long history of drug use and psychiatric symptoms, it will be difficult to accurately diagnose her mental illness. Her symptoms are consistent with major depression with psychotic features, schizoaffective disorder, and bipolar disorder. In addition, many of her psychiatric symptoms could be related to stimulant intoxication and/or withdrawal. Close monitoring of these symptoms will help to make a more accurate diagnosis. Medication changes can be made to address increases or decreases in symptoms. For example, an atypical antipsychotic would likely be appropriate for treating all of the above listed disorders. An SSRI antidepressant would be appropriate for treating major depression symptoms but could cause the onset of a manic episode if Tina were to have bipolar disorder. Ongoing psychiatric evaluation and care will need to occur. Motivational enhancement techniques will need to be continually used to help Tina to overcome her ambivalence and keep her engaged in the treatment process.

Justine

Justine is a thirty-five-year-old single Caucasian female. She grew up in a chaotic home environment. Her parents divorced when she was ten years old, and soon thereafter Justine began to experience a great deal of fear and anxiety. She experienced nightmares and was afraid to leave her mother for fear that something bad might happen to her. To cope with her anxiety, Justine developed several ritual behaviors such as organizing all of her toy dolls in a particular order and counting forward and backward to one hundred. As she grew older, she was still plagued with anxiety. She was preoccupied with cleanliness and was fearful of contracting a deadly disease. She would clean and reclean her house often into the wee hours of the night. At times her anxiety would be so great that she would have to leave work and go home, only to spend the rest of the day cleaning the house. When she was thirty-one, she went to her family doctor and told him about her "nervousness." He prescribed her xanax. Upon taking the xanax, Justine felt much better. She immediately felt less anxious and worried. After a while Justine noticed that the anxiety and worry would return within a few hours after she took the medication. She began to take the medication several times a day. Her doctor did prescribe the medication "as needed." She has now been taking the xanax several times per day for over four years. Her doctor did express some concern about the length of time she had been on the medication, but Justine convinced him that she was just too "nervous" to stop taking it. Just to be certain that she did not run out of the medication, Justine found an Internet site that would sell her the medication at a discounted rate. Even though she was taking a lot of the xanax, Justine would still experience periods of intense anxiety and worry. One day on the way home from work she experienced an overwhelming sense of panic. Her heart was racing and she had trouble breathing. Justine thought she was having a heart attack, so she went to the emergency room to be evaluated. After the emergency room physician determined that Justine was medically stable and not having a heart attack it was determined that she was likely having a panic attack. She was referred to an outpatient mental health clinic for evaluation and treatment.

Assessment and Treatment Issues

Justine kept her appointment at the mental health clinic. The clinician began her assessment interview. She was cross-trained in assessing and treating both mental health and substance abuse disorders. Justine presented as well groomed and appropriate in her appearance. She was slightly anxious. Justine described herself as a "nervous person." She went on to tell the clinician about her emergency room visit. The clinician asked if she had ever experienced anything like that before. Justine reported that she had not. As the clinician gathered more history, she asked Justine how long she had been feeling "nervous." Justine told the clinician, "as long as I can remember." As the clinician gathered Justine's history, it became clear that early on Justine experienced severe separation anxiety and developed compulsive and ritualistic behaviors to help relieve this anxiety. Justine continued to engage in obsessive and compulsive behaviors and thinking throughout her childhood and on into adulthood. Justine fits the criteria for the spectrum of anxiety disorders including obsessive-compulsive disorder and panic disorder. Since the clinician was cross-trained in assessing both mental health and substance use disorders, she was quick to notice that Justine had been on high doses of xanax for quite some time. While xanax is an appropriate medication for anxiety relief, long-term use of this substance, even as prescribed by a physician, can lead to physical and psychological dependency. The clinician also knew that sometimes as the medication is wearing off, the agitation and anxiety caused from the onset of withdrawal symptoms can be confused as a return of the original anxiety, thus reinforcing the need for more medication. Sometimes the anxiety and agitation can be severe enough to cause a person to think they are having a "heart attack" or some other serious medical problem. This is what is called a panic attack. The clinician suspected that Justine's panic attack may well have been the result of a combination of her anxiety disorders and her prolonged use of xanax. After further questioning, the clinician determined that Justine was concerned about her increasing use of xanax and had been trying to "cut down" on her own. The day of the panic attack she had only taken one dose in the morning and had not had any the rest of the day. Throughout the day she had become increasing nervous and agitated. She attributed that to her "nerves," and this only reinforced her need for the medication. As she was driving home from work, she was becoming more agitated and anxious and began to obsess about the medication, which she had left at home. Ultimately this resulted in the onset of her panic attack.

Treating Justine will be complicated by her physical and psychological dependence on xanax. Justine, on some level, was realizing that her xanax use was problematic, which is why she was trying to "cut down" her use. Because of her long-term use of this medication, she has developed an increased tolerance requiring more of the medication to get the same effect. Getting Justine to understand and accept that she has a "dependency" or addiction to this medication is the primary goal. Since Justine does not fit the pattern of an illicit drug abuser, it may be difficult to engage her in any traditional substance abuse treatment. Getting Justine referred to a physician trained in addiction medicine may be the best choice in order to determine how best to wean her off of the xanax without causing severe withdrawal and without exacerbating her anxiety symptoms. The physician may try to replace the xanax with a similar drug with a longer half life, such as klonipin. As they slowly decrease the amount of xanax, they will begin to increase the other medication. Once she is safely off of the xanax, they may start decreasing the klonipin or substitute other non-addictive medications. Several medications have been used to treat obsessive-compulsive disorder such as anafranil or most of the SSRI antidepressants.

Justine will also need to begin psychotherapy to focus on the underlying reasons for her anxiety and to help her gain control over her obsessive thinking and compulsive behaviors. Cognitive-behavioral therapy has been proven to be effective in treating anxiety disorders. An example would be helping Justine to identify her irrational beliefs related to her fear of contracting a deadly disease through the use of a "thought log" and teaching her alternative behaviors to replace the compulsive cleaning rituals, such as self-relaxation or moderate exercise. Used in conjunction with a revised medication regimen, these techniques should prove effective at helping Justine to relieve her anxiety and decrease her obsessive-compulsive behaviors.

Chapter Eight

Epilogue

Hopefully, as a seasoned clinician or a student in training, this book has given an overview of the most effective approaches and treatments for clients with co-occurring disorders. Practitioners in either substance abuse or mental health treatment settings should strive to become more proficient in assessing and treating these types of clients. While all treatment settings do not lend themselves to an integrated approach, clinicians of all disciplines should be aware of substance abuse and mental health resources in their areas and begin to create linkages and systems that are more integrated and multidisciplinary. Rather than allow the clients to navigate complex systems of care that may or may not be adequate or appropriate, practitioners should develop case management strategies that will assist the client as they move from provider to provider. Ideally, as programs become more integrated and practitioners become cross-trained, the client will experience a seamless process with the goal of "one stop shopping" for the majority of their treatment needs.

It is possible for the individual practitioner to become "integrated" in their philosophy and practice even if their agency or program is not. As more and more practitioners become versed in this philosophy and proficient in the evidence-based practices outlined in this book, it will force the larger systems of care to adjust and modify their practices. Such paradigm shifts are difficult and are often met with a great deal of resistance. A similar shift has been occurring during the past decade or so with the advent of managed health care. Practitioners have had to adjust their treatment philosophies and practices based upon the demands and requirements placed upon them by managed health care companies. While initially met with strong resistance, treatment providers and practitioners have had to adjust in order to survive. Currently there are several states that are beginning to create and fund treatment initiatives for integrated care of co-occurring disorders. Hopefully the important stakeholders will see the benefit of such treatment programs and create more funding and incentives toward moving in this direction.

For the individual practitioner, it is professionally and ethically his or her responsibility to receive the appropriate education and training in the assessment and treatment of co-occurring disorders. With the high prevalence of these disorders, it is a given that clinicians will encounter numerous clients with both a substance use and mental disorder. It is also a given that these clients will present themselves in all levels and types of treatment programs, social service venues, and legal services. Therefore, it is imperative for clinicians and administrators to develop linkages with agencies and providers who can administer the range of services that are necessary to engage, treat, and maintain clients with co-occurring disorders. By necessity this will require cooperation and coordination of services and funding streams. While this will be a painful and often daunting task, it must be done in order to provide more positive treatment outcomes. Many studies have shown that clients with co-occurring disorders are the highest utilizers of services throughout all systems (e.g., health care, social, legal) and as such, are the most expensive to manage. Rather than continue to provide costly and ineffective services to these clients, it would seem that it would be to everyone's benefit if there were a united and coordinated effort to target this population by expanding appropriate evidence-based treatments with a higher likelihood of positive treatment outcomes.

The role of case management, not necessarily as a "person" but as a function, becomes increasingly important with these clients. Because they require a broad range of services that are not always practical to provide even in an integrated program (e.g., housing, supported employment, medical), the practitioner is responsible for advocating and assisting the client with linkages to multiple resources. This takes time that clinicians with heavy caseloads may not have. It also takes knowledge of community resources. Just giving a client a phone number or a name and telling them to call an agency, service, or program is almost guaranteed to fail. For many clients with co-occurring disorders, the practitioner must either do the calling for or do it with the client in order to ensure that the linkage or referral occurs. For many, especially those in the substance abuse treatment field, this would sound like enabling the client. Philosophically it would be considered a bad practice. Certainly if a client is able and motivated to do something themselves, they should do it; however functional problems (e.g., cognitive deficits secondary to schizophrenia) may be present in many dually diagnosed clients that impair their ability to follow through and/or navigate complex systems or tasks. For many, it is a major accomplishment to remember to bathe on a regular basis. With this in mind, practitioners working with co-occurring disordered clients must be more active in the case management and referral process. This includes more "hand-holding" of the clients (e.g., transporting clients to appointments; following up with providers after appointments; and providing more detailed information on the front end of a referral). To accomplish this in a good way may require that clinicians working with these clients have reduced caseloads or that there be designated staff assigned primarily to case management activities.

Lastly, clinicians working with co-occurring disordered clients should seek out regular clinical supervision and case consultation, ideally in a multidisciplinary team environment. Individual practitioners should create virtual teams of providers, if possible, in order to collaborate and coordinate the care of these complex and often difficult clients. Clinicians working in agency and program settings may already be part of a treatment team but may lack the participation of various disciplines (e.g., clinicians in substance abuse treatment programs may be part of a team of substance abuse counselors but not have input from social workers, psychologists, and psychiatrists). The advantages of having the multiple disciplines represented on the treatment team are many, but the primary advantages are having a variety of perspectives and methodologies from which to gain input and the value of diversity of training and experiences. Good supervision and consultation contributes to the growth of everyone involved and usually leads to better treatment outcomes for the client. Unfortunately, the time for quality clinical supervision is often not allotted in the demand for "billable" time or paperwork completion. Not only is the lack of clinical supervision detrimental to clients, it is also detrimental to the well-being of the clinician. Clients with co-occurring disorders are the most difficult to treat and manage. They usually comprise the most demanding and frustrating cases. Without support and direction, the clinician can easily become disenchanted, disillusioned, and burned out. Turnover related to burnout and frustration in the helping professions is exceedingly high and in part can be attributed to the lack of ongoing clinical support and supervision.

In conclusion, co-occurring disorders are not a new phenomenon. They have existed forever. For many reasons the mental health and substance abuse fields along with society at large have separated problems from people. They have failed to look holistically at the person. Complex bureaucracies have evolved around treatment for problems rather than people. People are complex and may have many problems that coexist at the same time. Often when we treat a problem instead of a person, we fail to identify other concurrent problems that may exist and/or which may contribute to the one for which treatment is being rendered. This is not only costly in terms of time and money but is also costly in terms of lives left to wander the streets, crowd our jails, fill our institutions, and for many, fill our cemeteries. Continually repeating a behavior and expecting different results is said by some to be the definition of insanity. To continually provide ineffective, nonevidence-based treatments to clients with co-occurring disorders is not only unprofessional and unethical, but insane. As clinicians, students, and practitioners, it is our responsibility to get the training and education necessary to implement and practice these proven treatments for the betterment of our clients.

Bibliography

Albanese, M. J., and R. Pies. (2004). The bipolar patient with comorbid substance use disorder: Recognition and management. *CNS Drugs,* 18(9), 585–596.

Alcoholics Anonymous (AA) (1953). *The twelve steps and twelve traditions.* New York.

American Psychiatric Association (2000). *Diagnostic and statistical manual of mental disorders.* (4th ed.) text revision. Washington, DC.

Ball, S. A. (1998). Manualized treatment for substance abusers with personality disorders: Dual Focus Schema Therapy. *Addictive Behaviors,* 23(6), 883–891.

Ballasiotes, A. A., and T. L. Skaer. (2000). Use of lamotrigine in a patient with bipolar disorder and psychiatric comorbidity. *Clinical Therapeutics,* Sep. 22(9), 1146–1148.

Barrowclough, C., G. Haddock, N. Tarrier, S. Lewis, I. Moring, R. O'Brien, et al. (2001). Randomized controlled trial of motivational interviewing, cognitive behavioral therapy, and family intervention for patients with comorbid schizophrenia and substance use disorders. *American Journal of Psychiatry,* 158, 1706–1713.

Beck, A. T., and N. A. Rector. (2000). Cognitive therapy of schizophrenia. A new therapy for the new millennium. *American Journal of Psychotherapy,* 54, 291–300.

Beck, A. T., A. J. Rush, B. F. Shaw, and G. Emery. (1979). *Cognitive therapy of depression.* New York: The Guilford Press.

Beck, A. T., R. A. Steer, and G. K. Brown. (1996). *Beck Depression Inventory-II Manual.* San Antonio, TX: The Psychological Corporation.

Beck, A. T., F. D. Wright, C. F. Newman, and B. S. Liese. (1993). *Cognitive therapy of substance abuse.* New York: The Guilford Press.

Bellack, A. S., and C. C. DiClemente. (1999). Treating substance abuse among patients with schizophrenia. *Psychiatric Services,* 50, 75–80.

Bellack, A. S., and J. S. Gearon. (1998). Substance abuse treatment for people with schizophrenia. *Addictive Behavior,* 23(6), 749–766.

Bellack, A. S., K. T. Mueser, S. Gingerich, and J. Agresta. (1997). *Social skills training for schizophrenia: A step by step guide.* New York: The Guilford Press.

Brady, K. T., D. E. Grice, L. Dustan, and C. Randall. (1993). Gender differences in substance use disorders. *American Journal of Psychiatry,* 150(11), 1707–1711.

Brady, K. T., T. K. Killeen, T. Brewerton, and J. S. Lucerini. (2000). Comorbidity of psychiatric disorders and posttraumatic stress disorder. *Journal of Clinical Psychiatry,* 61, (Suppl.7), 22–32.

Brady, K. T., S. C. Sonne, R. J. Malcolm, C. L. Randall, K. Simpson, B. S. Dansky, et al. (2002). Carbamazepine in the treatment of cocaine dependence: Subtyping by affective disorder. *Experimental Clinical Psychopharmacology,* 10, 276–285.

Breslau, N. (2004). Daily smoking and the subsequent onset of psychiatric disorders. *Psychological Medicine,* 34, 323–333.

Brewer, C. (1992). Controlled trials of Antabuse in alcoholism: The importance of supervision and adequate dosage. *Acta Psychiatrica Scandinavica,* 86, 51–58.

Brooks, A. J., and P. E. Penn. (2003). Comparing treatments for dual diagnosis: Twelve-step and self-management and recovery training. *The American Journal of Drug and Alcohol Abuse.* 29(2), 359–383.

Carroll, K. M. (2004). Behavioral therapies for co-occurring substance use and mood disorders. *Biological Psychiatry,* 56, 778–784.

Carey, K. B., M. P. Carey, S. A. Maisto, and D. M. Purnine. (2002). The feasibility of enhancing psychiatric outpatient's readiness to change their substance use. *Psychiatric Services,* 53(5), 602–608.

Carey, K. B., D. M. Purnine, S. A. Maisto, M. P. Carey, and J. S. Simons. (2000). Treating substance abuse in the context of severe and persistent mental illness: Clinician's perspectives. *Journal of Substance Abuse Treatment,* 19, 189–198.

Center for Substance Abuse Treatment (CSAT). (1994). *Simple screening instruments for outreach for alcohol and other drug abuse and infectious diseases.* Treatment Improvement Protocol (TIP) Series 11. DHHS Publication No. (SMA) 94-2094. Rockville, MD: SAMHSA.

Center for Substance Abuse Treatment (CSAT). (2004). *Substance abuse treatment for persons with co-occurring disorders.* Treatment Improvement Protocol Series (TIP), Number 42. Rockville, MD: SAMHSA.

Clodfelter, R. C., M. J. Albanese, G. Baker, K. Domoto, A. Gui, and E. J. Khantizian. (2003). The MICA case conference program at Tewksbury Hospital, MA: An integrated treatment model. *American Journal on Addictions,* 12, 448–454.

Conley, R. R., D. L. Kelly, and E. A. Gale. (1998). Olanzapine response in treatment-refractory schizophrenic patients with a history of substance abuse. *Schizophrenia Research,* 33, 95–101.

Donnelly, J., M. Rosenbert, and W. Fleeson. (1970). The evolution of the mental status—past and future. *American Journal of Psychiatry,* 125, 997–1002.

Drake, R. E., S. M. Essock, A. Shaner, K. B. Carey, K. Minkoff, and L. Kola, et.al. (2001). Implementing dual diagnosis services for clients with severe mental illness. *Psychiatric Services,* 52(4), 469–476.

Drake, R. E., H. H. Goldman, H. S. Leff, A. F. Lehman, L. Dixon, K. T. Mueser, and W. C. Torrey. (2001). Implementing evidenced-based practices in routine mental health service settings. *Psychiatric Services,* 52(2), 179–182.

Drake, R. E., G. J. McHugo, and D. L. Noordsy. (1993). Treatment of alcoholics among schizophrenic outpatients: Four-year outcomes. *American Journal of Psychiatry,* 150, 328–329.

Drake, R. E., K. T. Mueser, M. F. Brunette, and G. J. McHugo (2004). A review of treatments for people with severe mental illness and co-occurring substance abuse disorders. *Psychiatric Rehabilitation Journal,* 27(4), 360–374.

Drake, R. E., and M. A. Wallach. (1993). Moderate drinking among people with severe mental illness. *Hospital and Community Psychiatry,* 54, 700–705.

Drake, R. E., and M. A. Wallach. (2000). Dual diagnosis: Fifteen years of progress. *Psychiatric Services,* 51, 1126–1129.

Drake, R. E., H. Xie, G. J. McHugo, and A. I. Green. (2000). The effects of clozapine on alcohol and drug use disorders among schizophrenic patients. *Schizophrenic Bulletin,* 26, 441–449.

Drake, R. E., H. Xie, G. J. McHugo, and M. Shumbay. (2004). Three year outcomes of long-term patients with co-occurring bipolar and substance use disorders. *Biological Psychiatry,* 56, 749–756.

Ewing, J. A. (1984). Detecting alcoholism, The CAGE questionnaire. *Journal of American Medical Association,* 252(14), 1905–1907.

Folstein, M. F., S. E. Folstein, and P. R. McHugh. (1975). Mini-mental state: A practical method for grading the cognitive state patients for the clinician. *Journal of Psychiatric Research,* 12, 189–198.

Gassman, R. A., H. W. Demone, Jr., and R. Albilal. (2001). Alcohol and other drug content in core courses: Encouraging substance abuse assessment. *Journal of Social Work Education,* 9, 12–24.

Gavin, D. R., H. E. Ross, and H. A. Skinner. (1989). Diagnostic validity of the Drug Abuse Screening Test in the assessment of DSM-III drug disorders. *British Journal of Addiction,* 84(3), 301–307.

Gil-Rivas, V., R. Fiorentine, and M. D. Anglin. (1996). Sexual abuse, physical abuse, and posttraumatic stress disorder among women participants in outpatient drug abuse treatment. *Journal of Psychoactive Drugs,* 28(1), 95–102.

Gold, M. S. (1994). Marijuana. In *Principles of addiction medicine,* ed. N. S. Miller and M. C. Doot (sec. 2, chap. 8, pp. 1–6), Chevy Chase, MD: American Society of Addiction Medicine.

Goldsmith, R. J., and V. Garlapati. (2004). Behavioral interventions for dual-diagnosis patients. *Psychiatric Clinics of North America,* Dec. 27(4), 709–725.

Graeber, D. A., T. B. Moyers, G. Griffith, E. Guajardo, and S. Tonigan. (2003). A pilot study comparing motivational interviewing and an educational intervention in patients with schizophrenia and alcohol use disorders. *Community Mental Health Journal,* 39(3), 189–202.

Granholm, E., R. Anthenelli, R. Monterio, J. Sevicile, and M. Stoler. (2003). Brief integrated outpatient dual-diagnosis treatment reduces psychiatric hospitalizations. *The American Journal on Addictions,* 12, 306–313.

Hamilton, T., and P. Samples. (1995).*The Twelve Steps and Dual Disorders Workbook.* Center City, MN: Hazelden Publications.

Handmaker, N. S., W. R. Miller, and M. Manicke. (1999). Findings of a pilot study of motivational interviewing with pregnant drinkers. *Journal of Studies On Alcohol,* 60, 285–287.

Hester, R. K., and W. R. Miller. (eds.) (1995). *Handbook of alcoholism treatment approaches: Effective alternatives* (2nd. ed.). Needham, MA: The Guilford Press.

Ho, A. P., J. W. Tsuang, R. P. Liberman, R. Wang, J. N. Wilkins, T. A. Eckman, and A. L. Shaner. (1999). Achieving effective treatment of patients with chronic psychotic illness and comorbid substance dependence. *American Journal of Psychiatry,* 156(11), 1765–1770.

Jaffe, J. H. (1980). Drug addiction and drug abuse. In *Goodman and Gilman's: The pharmacological basis of therapeutics*, ed. A. G. Gilman, L. S. Goodman, and A. Gilman. New York: Macmillan.

Jerrell, J. M., and M. S. Ridgely. (1999). Impact of robustness of program implementation on outcomes of clients in dual diagnosis programs. *Psychiatric Services,* 50, 109–112.

Kavanaugh, D. J., L. Greenway, L. Jenner, J. B. Saunders, A. White, J. Sorban, and G. Hamilton. (2000). Contrasting views and experiences of health professionals on the management of comorbid substance misuse and mental disorders. *Australian and New Zealand Journal of Psychiatry and Law,* 34, 279–289.

Keltner, N. L., and D. G. Folks. (2005). *Psychotropic Drugs.* St. Louis, MO: Elsevier.

Kessler, R. C. (2004). The epidemiology of dual diagnosis. *Biological Psychiatry,* 56, 730–737.

Kessler, R. C., R. M. Crum, L. A. Warner, C. B. Nelson, J. Schulenberg, and J. C. Anthony. (1997). Lifetime co-occurrence of DSM-III-R alcohol abuse and dependence with other psychiatric disorders in the National Comorbidity Survey. *Archives of General Psychiatry,* 54, 313–321.

Laudet, A. B., S. Magura, C. M. Cleland, H. S. Vogel, E. L. Knight, and A. Rosenblum. (2004). The effect of 12-step based fellowship participation on abstinence among dually diagnosed persons: A two year longitudinal study. *Journal of Psychoactive Drugs,* 36(2), 207–216.

Levin, F. R., and G. Hennessy. (2004). Bipolar disorder and substance abuse. *Biological Psychiatry,* 56, 738–748.

Linehan, M. M., H. Schmidt III, L. A. Dimeff, J. C. Craft, J. Kanter, and K. A. Comtois. (1999). Dialectical behavior therapy for patients with borderline personality disorder and drug-dependence. *American Journal on Addictions,* 8(4), 279–292.

Marshall, K., and F. Deane. (2004). General practitioner's detection and management of patients with a dual diagnosis: Implications for education and training. *Drug and Alcohol Review,* Dec. 23(4), 455–462.

Maslin, J., H. L. Graham, M. Cawley, A. Copello, M. Birchwood, G. Gerogiou, D. McGovern, K. Mueser, and J. Orford. (2001). Combined severe mental health and substance use problems: What are the training and support needs of staff working with this client group? *Journal of Mental Health,* 10, 131–140.

McLellan, A. T., D. Carise, and H. D. Kleber. (2003). The national addiction treatment infrastructure: Can it support the public's demand for quality care? *Journal of Substance Abuse Treatment,* 78, 125–129.

McLellan, A. T., H. Kushner, D. Metzger, R. Peters, L. Smith, G. Grissom, H. Petti-nati, and M. Argeriou. (1992). The fifth edition of the Addiction Severity Index. *Journal of Substance Abuse Treatment,* 9(3), 199–213.

McLellan, A. T., and K. Meyers. (2004). Contemporary addiction treatment: A review of systems problems for adults and adolescents. *Biological Psychiatry,* 56, 764–770.

Miklowitz, D. J. (2004). Psychosocial therapies in bipolar disorder. *Current Psychosis and Therapeutics Reports,* 2, 142–146.

Miller, W. R., and S. Rollnick. (2002). *Motivational Interviewing: Preparing People for Change.* (2nd ed.) New York: The Guilford Press.

Minkoff, K. (2000). An integrated model for the management of co-occurring psychiatric and substance abuse disorders in managed care systems. *Disease Management Health Outcomes,* Nov. 8(5), 251–257.

Minkoff, K. (1989). An integrated treatment model for dual diagnosis of psychosis and addiction. *Hospital and Community Psychiatry,* 40, 1031–1036.

Monti, P. M., R. M. Kadden, D. J. Rossenow, N. L. Cooney, and D. B. Abrams. (2002). *Treating alcohol dependence: A coping skills training guide* (2nd ed.). New York: The Guilford Press.

Mueser, K. T., and S. R. McGurk. (2004). Schizophrenia. *Lancet,* 363, 2063–2072.

Mueser, K. T., D. L. Noordsy, R. E. Drake, and L. Fox. (2003). *Integrated Treatment for Dual Disorders.* New York: The Guilford Press.

Mueser, K. T., D. L. Noordsy, L. Fox, and R. Wolfe. (2003). Disulfiram treatment for alcoholism in severe mental illness. *American Journal of Addictions,* 12, 242–253.

Mueser, K. T., S. D. Rosenberg, R. E. Drake, K. M. Miles, G. Wolford, R. Vidaves, and K. Carrieri. (1999). Conduct disorder, antisocial personality disorder, and substance use disorders in schizophrenia and major affective disorders. *Journal of Studies on Alcohol,* 60, 278–284.

Mueser, K. T., W. C. Torrey, D. Lynde, P. Singer, and R. E. Drake. (2003). Implementing evidence-based practices for people with severe mental illness. *Behavior Modification,* 27, 387–411.

Myrick, H., J. Culver, S. Swavely, and H. Peters. (2004). Diagnosis and treatment of co-occurring affective disorders and substance use disorders. *Psychiatric Clinics of North America,* 27(4).

Noordsy, D. L., B. Schwab, L. Fox, and R. E. Drake. (1996). The role of self-help programs in the rehabilitation of persons with severe mental illness and substance use disorders. *Community Mental Health Journal,* 32, 71–81.

Nunes, E. V., and F. R. Levin. (2004). Treatment of depression in patient's wit alcohol or other drug dependence: A meta-analysis. *Journal of the American Medical Association,* 291(5), 1887–1896.

Osher, F. C., and L. L. Kofoed. (1989). Treatment of patients with psychiatric and psychoactive substance use disorders. *Hospital and Community Psychiatry,* 40, 1025–1030.

Penn, P. E., and A. J. Brooks. (2000). Five years, twelve steps, and REBT in the treatment of dual diagnosis. *Journal of Rational-Emotive and Cognitive-Behavior Therapy,* 18(4), 197–208.

Perkinson, R. (2002). *Chemical Dependency Counseling* (2nd ed.). Thousand Oaks, CA: Sage Publications.

Pettinati, H. M. (2004). Antidepressant treatment of co-occurring depression and alcohol dependence. *Biological Psychiatry,* 56, 785–792.

Prochaska, J. K., and C. C. DiClemente. (1984). *The trans-theoretical approach: Crossing the traditional boundaries of therapy.* Homewood, IL: Dow-Jones/ Irwin.

RachBeisel, J., J. Scott, and L. Dixon. (1999). Co-occurring severe mental illness and substance use disorders: A review of recent research. *Psychiatric Services,* 50, 1427–1434.

Reiger, D. A., M. E. Farmer, D. S. Rae, B. Z. Lacke, S. J. Keith, L. L. Judd, and F. K. Goodwin. (1990). Co-morbidity of mental disorders with alcohol and other drug abuse: Results from the Epidemiological Catchment Area (ECA) study. *Journal of the American Medical Association,* 264, 2511–2518.

Ridgely, M. S., F. C. Osher, H. H. Goldman, and J. A. Talbott. (1987). *Executive summary: Chronic mentally ill young adults with substance abuse problems: A review of research, treatment, and training issues.* Baltimore, MD: Mental Health Services Research Center, University of Maryland School of Medicine.

Ries, R., and Consensus Panel (1994). *Assessment and treatment of patients with co-existing mental illness and alcohol and other drug abuse.* Treatment Improvement Protocol (TIP) Series No. 9 (No. SMA-94-2078), Washington, DC: DHHS Publications.

Roberts, L. J., A. Shaner, and T. A. Eckman. (1999). *Overcoming addictions: Skills training for people with schizophrenia.* New York: W.W. Norton.

Rogers, C. R. (1951). *Client-centered therapy.* Boston: Houghton-Mifflin.

Salloum, I. M., J. R. Cornelius, M. E. Thase, D. C. Daley, L. Kirisci, and C. Spotts. (1998). Naltrexone utility in depressed alcoholics. *Psychopharmacology Bulletin,* 34, 111–115.

Sass, H., M. Soyka, K. Mann, and W. Zieglgansberger. (1996). Relapse prevention by Acamprosate: Results from a placebo-controlled study on alcohol dependence. *Archives of General Psychiatry,* 53, 673–680.

Selzer, M. L. (1971). The Michigan Alcoholism Screening Test: The quest for a new diagnostic instrument. *American Journal of Psychiatry,* 127(12), 1653–1658.

Trimpey, J. (1996). *Rational Recovery: The New Cure for Substance Addiction.* New York: Pocket Books.

Velasquez, M. M., G. G. Maurer, C. Crouch, and C. C. DiClemente. (2001). *Group treatment for substance abuse: A stages of change therapy manual.* New York: The Guilford Press.

Watkins, T. R., A. Lewellen, and M. C. Barrett. (2001). *Dual Diagnosis: An integrated approach to treatment.* Thousand Oaks, CA: Sage Publications.

Weiss, R. D., M. L. Griffin, S. F. Greenfield, L. M. Najavits, D. Wyner, and J. A. Soto. (2000). Group therapy for patients with bipolar disorder and substance dependence: Results of a pilot study. *Journal of Clinical Psychiatry,* 61, 361–367.

Weiss, R. D., M. Kolodziej, M. L. Griffin, L. M. Najavits, L. M. Jacobson, and S. F. Greenfield. (2004). Substance use and perceived symptom improvement among patients with bipolar disorder and substance dependence. *Journal of Affective Disorders,* 79, 279–283.

Weiss, R. D., L. M. Najavits, and S. F. Greenfield. (1999). A relapse prevention group for patients with bipolar and substance use disorders. *Journal of Substance Abuse Treatment,* 16, 47–54.

Wilens, T. E., S. V. Faraone, J. Biedirman, and S. Gunawardine. (2003). Does stimulant therapy of attention-deficit/hyperactivity disorder beget later substance abuse?: A meta-analytic review of the literature. *Pediatrics,* 111, 179–185.

Xie, H., G. J. McHugo, B. S. Helmstetter, and R. E. Drake (in press). Three year recovery outcomes for patients with co-occurring schizophrenia and substance use disorders. *Schizophrenia Research,* 51, 141–166.

Ziedonis, D. M. (2004). Integrated treatment of co-occurring mental illness and addiction: Clinical intervention, program, and system perspectives. *CNS Spectrum,* 9(12), 892–904.

Ziedonis, D. M., and K. Trudeau. (1997). Motivation to quit using substances among individuals with schizophrenia: Implications for a motivation-based treatment model. *Schizophrenia Bulletin,* 23, 229–238.

Zweben, J. E., and D. E. Smith. (1989). Considerations in using psychotropic medication with dual diagnosis patients in recovery. *Journal of Psychoactive Drugs,* 21(2), 221–226.

Index

About the Author

John K. Smith is a licensed psychotherapist with over twenty-five years of experience in the mental health and chemical dependency fields. He is the program administrator for the Dual Diagnosis Day Treatment Program at Doctor's Hospital of West Covina, California, and a therapist in private practice. In addition, Dr. Smith is a professor of Alcohol and Drug Counseling at Mt. San Antonio College in Walnut, Calfornia. Dr. Smith holds a Ph.D. in Addictions from International University for Graduate Studies and a master's degree in Social Work from Indiana University. He is a California Licensed Clinical Social Worker.

Date Due

JAN 2 8 2009		
Feb 25 09		
Mar 25 09		
MAR 2 0 2009		
APR 1 5 2009		
May 14 2009		
MAY 1 4 2009		
MAY 1 4 2009		

BRODART, CO.   Cat. No. 23-233-003   Printed in U.S.A.